BERLITZ®

AUSTRALIA

1988/1989 Edition

W9-ANO-320

By the staff of Berlitz Guides
A Macmillan Company

How to use our guide

These 256 pages cover the **highlights of Australia,** grouped by state. Although not exhaustive, our selection of sights will enable you to make the best of your trip.

The **sights** to see are contained between pages 38 and 189. Those most highly recommended are pinpointed by the Berlitz traveller symbol.

The **Where to Go** section on page 36 will help you plan your visit according to the time available.

For **general background** see the sections Australia and the Australians (p. 8), Facts and Figures (p. 19), History (p. 20) and Historical Landmarks (p. 34).

Entertainment and **activities** (including eating out) are described between pages 190 and 216.

The **practical information,** hints and tips you will need before and during your trip begin on page 218. This section is arranged alphabetically with a list for easy reference.

The **map section** at the back of the book (pp. 241–251) will help you find your way around and locate the principal sights.

Finally, if there is anything you cannot find, look in the complete **index** (pp. 252–256).

CONTENTS

CONTENTS

Text:	Ken Bernstein
Staff Editor:	Barbara Ender
Layout:	Doris Haldemann
Photography:	Claude Huber
	p. 24 Barry Skipsey, N.T. Tourist Commission;
	pp. 123, 133, 135, 156 John Hawkes, Sydney;
	pp. 158–159, 161, 163, 180, 183, 187, 188
	Wildlight, Sydney
Drawings:	Max Thommen
Cartography:	Falk Falk-Verlag, Hamburg
	pp. 6–7, 38, 63, 70, 94, 122, 142, 162, 179
	Max Thommen

Acknowledgements
We would like to thank Sigrid Henrich, of the Australian Tourist Commission in Frankfurt, and Nicholas Campbell, for their invaluable help in the preparation of this guide.

Found an error or an omission in this Berlitz Guide? Or a change or new feature we should know about? Our editor would be happy to hear from you, and a postcard would do. Be sure to include your name and address, since in appreciation for a useful suggestion, we'd like to send you a free travel guide.

Although we make every effort to ensure the accuracy of all the information in this book, changes occur incessantly. We cannot therefore take responsibility for facts, prices, addresses and circumstances in general that are constantly subject to alteration.

Cover photo: Sydney Harbour

0   200   400 km.

0   200   400 miles

N

INDIAN   OCEAN

Broome

Kimberle

Port Hedland

Great Sandy

Desert

Carnarvon

Geraldton

Kalgoorlie ○   *Nullarbo*

Perth
Fremantle

Bunbury

Esperance   *Grea*

Albany

SOUTHERN

AUSTRALIA AND THE AUSTRALIANS

Down Under has always seemed bizarre: an unbelievably distant, flat landscape supporting off-colour trees, grizzled prospectors and absurd if lovable animals. In Queen Victoria's heyday, a character in an Oscar Wilde play summed up the foreigner's blurred impression of Australia: "It must be so pretty with all the dear little kangaroos flying about. Agatha has found it on the map."

The preconception hasn't changed much in a century. Australia still appears to be the most curious upside-down continent; and not only the kangaroos but the people sound a bit frivolous, what with everybody sunbathing, surfing and swilling beer all the time.

Like most clichés, there's something in it. The Australians are fanatics of the outdoor life. They radiate rude health and tanned muscles. If they're not actually at the beach, they're probably hiking, jogging or playing football, or out in the garden barbecuing slabs of beef. In hand: an icy beer to pacify the fiercest thirst. The Australians are not quite the world's most insatiable beer drinkers, but they're working on it.

Prospectors seeking gold or other minerals still roam the Outback, where life is hard. Remote cattle farms are so big that cowboys conduct their roundups by helicopter; one of the ranches is about the size of Belgium. As an environment, the Outback is as inhospitable as a rock. The people of the Outback, appropriately, are hard as rock, apparently immune to sunstroke and flood, snakebite and crocodile nip.

Life in the bush may be the stereotype, but camping holidays are as close as the overwhelming majority of citizens ever get to it. The average Australian today is a confirmed city-slicker. About 70 per cent of the population lives in the ten biggest cities. Few Australians have ever seen a koala dozing in a eucalyptus tree or a kangaroo suckling her joey—except at the zoo.

In the childhood of the earth, Australia was land-linked to India, Africa and Antarctica. The planet's growing pains and continental drift broke up the conglomeration, the oceans intervened, and eternities of isolation ensued. Plants and animals, cut off from the evolutionary mainstream, developed in exotic ways that were to engross generations

Rugged independence lights the face of an Outback old-timer.

of scientists and ordinary tourists.

The only humans sharing the continent with the native animals were nomadic Aboriginal tribes. These first Australians, Stone Age people, inventors of the round-trip boomerang, are thought to have arrived from Asia perhaps 40,000 years ago. Everything went smoothly until the 18th century, when British convicts were shipped out to colonize Australia on behalf of King George III.

The dark-skinned hunters may have numbered 300,000 at the time the British Empire casually seized their traditional lands; now the Aboriginal population is about half that. No easy answers have been found for their problems of adjustment to the white society around them, but the

government is trying hard to right a lengthy list of age-old wrongs.

The fact that the construction of modern Australia was begun by chain gangs of convicted felons rather than firm-jawed idealists was bound to affect the national psyche. Does this quirk of history explain why Australians are defensive about their country, asking foreigners what they think about it, then waiting anxiously for the answer? Does the family tree account for the cockneyesque brand of English they speak? Is today's social mobility and sense of egalitarianism a reaction to those early days of keepers and convicts, rulers and ruled? Does the

Uluru, or "meeting place", revered by the Aborigines for centuries.

macho tradition stem from the scarcity of female companionship in the young colony?

Australia's geographical superlatives are clear-cut: it's the earth's biggest island. More accurately, call it the smallest and least populous (16 million) of the continents, but the only one housing a single nation. Australia occupies about as much space as the 48 mainland states of the U.S., or 24 times the area of the British Isles. Something to think about when you plan your See-Australia-in-a-Hurry itinerary.

Another claim for the record book: Australia is the flattest continent. Having had plenty of time to be worn down, the ancient terrain hardly ever rises above middle-ranking hilltops. But the nation's summit, Mount Kosciusko (elevation 2,228 metres —7,316 feet), is almost as high as Mexico City. You can ski in the Australian Alps in August. But if snowdrifts are too heady a prospect, you can come down to earth at salty Lake Eyre, the continent's lowest point, 16 metres (39 feet) below sea level. It is almost always bone dry.

Australia is the driest continent, the mass of its interior a blotter of desert, a parched rebuff to all but the most dauntless pioneers. Although the Murray River and its tributaries add up to a Mississippi or a Yangtse

in length, few other Australian rivers rate much more than a rowing boat. And many of the refreshing blue squiggles on maps are just sand traps for at least part of the year.

The coastline is the least ruffled of all the continents, a circumference of 36,735 kilometres (almost 23,000 miles) devoted to sweeping beaches rather than coves and creeks. Here you can dip a toe, or a surfboard, in legendary seas and oceans, among them the Coral Sea, the Timor Sea, the Indian Ocean and the Southern Ocean.

Australia is a long way from familiar climes: 6,000 miles from the United States, 11,000 from Britain. Much more distant in cultural terms are Australia's nearest neighbours, Indonesia and Papua New Guinea, only a kangaroo's hop to the north. The Asian connection is becoming ever more important, politically, economically and in human terms; a look at the faces on any city street shows the vastly increased flow of immigrants from the Pacific.

But European influences still dominate in spite of the dilution of the original British character of the country. The Australian melting pot now contains a savoury mixture of fish and chips, spaghetti, souvlaki and sauerkraut ... and portions of Peking duck and Vietnamese

Sea, surf, sun and fun—
an Australian love affair.

spring rolls. Don't be surprised if you hear radio programmes in Arabic or even Welsh.

At almost all latitudes of Australia's sprawl from rainforest and mangrove swamp through fertile farmland to snowy peaks, you'll see hardy trees of two main families. More than 500 types of eucalyptus, mostly grey-green, are native to Australia, and 600 species of flowering acacia are at home. They look scrubby but brave where the earth is chronically thirsty, robust in nicer neighbourhoods. Unromantically terse, the Australians call eucalyptus "gum" and acacia "wattle", making them sound rather like wizened bushes with poisonous berries. But by any alias, gum and wattle

13

remain noble, useful and often beautiful. Closer to the ground, wild flowers as vivid as desert pea and kangaroo paw thrive on the morning dew.

Australia's animals are as odd as they are charming. Australia has a virtual monopoly on monotremes. The generic name for these most primitive of all mammals may not ring a bell, but you'll recognize the individual exhibits—the spiny anteater and the platypus, a compromise between a bird, a reptile and a mammal. More familiar are the marsupials, with pouches to solve the baby-sitting problem. Bounding across the landscape are dozens of varieties of kangaroo, from pocket-sized wallabies to giant red roos big enough to cow any heavyweight boxer. Another marsupial, the adorable koala, eschews violent exercise, spending its days drowsing in a eucalyptus haze.

Birdwatchers can count hundreds of species. Thrillingly colourful birds are as common as sparrows, and lyrical or humorous bird-calls provide every evening's country music. The indigenous stars have names like flowerpecker, honeyeater and kookaburra, but the favourite bird of crossword puzzlers, the emu, can't sing—or fly.

Divers go down under Down Under to admire the sort of fish you see in a collector's tropical tank—but in these seas they're ten times bigger. Gorgeous angel fish and moorish idols glide past the enthralled skin diver's mask. Big-mouthed sharks and venomous scorpion fish may also turn up, but they are subjects for more serious study.

For enthusiasts of underwater spectacles, the most exciting place in the world is the Great Barrier Reef. This 1,200-mile-long miracle—a living structure of coral—thrills the imagination in its immensity and in the intricate detail of brightly hued organisms shaped like antlers, flowers, fans or brains. The most sublime tropical fish congregate there, too.

The reef, one of Australia's top priority tourist destinations, has become ever more accessible. So has Ayers Rock, with its own airport and hotel complex. Australia's highly developed transport system puts the whole continent within reach: beaches and ski resorts, dynamic cities and Outback ghost towns.

Considering the country's admittedly out-of-the-way location, it's remarkable that tourism has become the single biggest industry. More than a million foreign tourists a year head for Australia. The visitors appreciate the friendly welcome, the civilized facilities and the agreeable climate. The most popular tourist corridor slices through the south-east corner of the country, where there's a choice of big cities, beaches and bush.

Sydney, the brash, brassy city where the history of Australia began, is no more typical of the country than Manhattan is representative of America. But the setting is sensational, and you only have to travel beyond the suburbs to see your first "Caution—Kangaroos" sign.

The rival metropolis, Melbourne, has a Chicago dynamism, grandiose business buildings, and more than its share of parks. Add sophisticated shopping, eating and nightlife, and the city's capricious weather seems less of a drawback.

To avoid political friction, the federal capital was built on neutral ground between Sydney and Melbourne. The result, Canberra, is a forested exercise in town planning, with enough crescents, circles and curving roads to baffle Henry the Navigator.

The other sizeable cities, which double as state capitals, share a clean, relaxed air: gracious, parklike Adelaide and Perth; sunny, subtropical Brisbane; and the most modern of towns, the reborn Darwin. Hobart, the brisk and tidy capital of Tasmania, is a seafarers' haven.

Notwithstanding the charm of the cities, most visitors search for the "real" Australia in the Outback, a land of rocky hills, desert or rainforest ... and adventure. When you imagine the Middle of Nowhere, Back of Beyond, the Never-Never, this is the place. The entire population of the Northern Territory—a land about the size of France, Spain and Italy combined—fits into a phone book with 81 pages of alphabetical listings. Most of the total area of Australia is occupied by similarly vacant wilderness. You drive for hours to the next town on the map and discover it's no more than a pub with a petrol pump. No wonder the Aussies are so friendly!

Among the less obvious things tourists come to see are the country's other industries. Visiting a "station"—a cattle ranch or sheep farm—is seeing the Australian myth come to life. Some tourists arrange fossicking expeditions—freelance digging for gold or opals. Others get to look down on an enormous open-cast bauxite mine or descend the shaft into the claustrophobic mysteries of a gold mine.

Putting the country's mineral resources into perspective, Australia is the world's No. 1 exporter of coal, the biggest producer of bauxite, and in the top international rank when it comes to mining iron, lead, zinc,

Pages 16–17: Moments of reflection on the concrete and the green.

uranium and diamonds. Above ground, grazing land predominates, and the sheep outnumber the people by about ten to one. Australia is the world leader in wool production. Its farms also supply many countries with meat, dairy products, wheat, sugar and fruit.

Yet, contrary to its timeless rural image, Australia today is a highly industrialized urban society. Factories turn out everything from ships to chips. The trend, though, is unmistakably towards the service sector—trade, community services and construction. The labour force is highly unionized, and salaries are above the level known in most countries. Prices, too, are high.

Until recent times, Australia was strictly a man's world, where the missus stayed at home scrubbing the floor while the head of the household played football with the gang, talked macho, and drank and drank. The most popular Australian poet, Henry Lawson, explained all this drinking as "a man's way of crying". More liberal drinking laws have made things less desperate. The gender gulf, too, has narrowed. Liberated women are now seen almost everywhere in the mainstream of society, though some areas of awkwardness persist.

Americans tend to find Australia quite English, while British visitors are reminded of America. The informality and pioneering spirit Down Under do recall the American style, while the social and economic preoccupations—and the attitudes towards food—more often take after the British model. The Australian language may occasionally baffle English-speakers from almost anywhere, but it's admirably ingenious, and as good-humoured as the Aussies themselves.

As for culture, the average Australian might find the word itself rather tedious, maintaining that television and sports are culture enough. But don't you bet on it, mate! Go to any bookstore, or one of the imposing arts centres ... or to any theatre showing a locally produced play or film. All along a varied, challenging front, Australian creativity is thriving.

The federal government pours millions of dollars a year into the arts; so do the states. It shows up in the vigorous design of the new museums and opera houses, in the high calibre of the performing artists and the enthusiasm of the audiences. For the tourist it means the chance to see treasures of art along with nature's wonders, leaping ballerinas as well as kangaroos. This is the place to soak up some rays, and life and lore and marvels galore. There's more to Australia than its sunny disposition.

FACTS AND FIGURES

Geography: Area 7,682,300 square kilometres (2,966,150 square miles), about the size of the continental United States. Nearest neighbours: Indonesia, Papua New Guinea, Solomons, Fiji and New Zealand. Highest point: Mount Kosciusko, 2,228 metres (7,316 feet); lowest: Lake Eyre, 16 metres (39 feet) below sea level.

Population: About 16 million. One person in four is either an immigrant or the child of an immigrant. About 1 per cent of the population is Aboriginal.

Capital: Canberra (population 265,000)

Major Cities: Sydney (3,356,000), Melbourne (2,889,000), Brisbane (1,200,000), Adelaide (979,000), Perth (983,000).

Government: Democratic federal constitutional monarchy: Queen Elizabeth II is formally Queen of Australia, represented by a governor-general. Federal government is headed by the prime minister, who is leader of the elected parliamentary majority. Other levels of government: state governments and legislatures, and municipal administrations. There are six states and two mainland territories—the Australian Capital Territory (A.C.T.) and Northern Territory, which has been self-governing since 1978. Voting is compulsory in federal elections for everyone except the Aborigines, who can choose whether or not to register. If they register, they are obliged to vote.

Economy: Australia is a leading exporter of beef, lamb, wool, wheat, bauxite, nickel, coal, iron ore. Inflation, unemployment and the balance of trade give cause for concern.

Religion: More than three-quarters of Australians who claim a religion are Christians, mostly Anglicans and Roman Catholics. There are also significant Jewish, Islamic and Buddhist communities.

Language: English with colourful antipodal embroidery.

HISTORY

Quibble if you will over the date, but Dreamtime certainly goes back a very long way. Some authorities believe the first inhabitants of Australia arrived 40,000 years ago; others go off the deep end and suggest it may have been 80,000 years earlier.

What started the migrations must have been the Ice Age, which encouraged the shivering cave dwellers of the northern hemisphere to head for the sun belt. This set off a chain reaction, forcing more southerly folk out of their way. As titanic ice caps accumulated, sea levels dropped drastically, revealing land bridges from island to island, or at least reducing the distances to be sailed. Most of the route from the Asian mainland to Australia would have been walkable or wadeable.

So, searching for greener pastures or more elbow room, or escaping from war or vendetta —or perhaps blown off course on what should have been a routine voyage—the original immigrants arrived Down Under. The first Australians had little problem adapting to the new environment. As Stone Age hunters and food gatherers, they were accustomed to foraging, and the takings in the new continent were good: plenty of fish, berries and roots, and, for a change of diet, why not just spear a kangaroo?

"Dreamtime" is the all-purpose name for everything that came before. It puts Aboriginal history, traditions and culture under one mythological roof. Dreamtime's version of Genesis recounts how ancestral heroes created the stars, the earth and all the creatures. Dreamtime explains why the animals, insects and plants are the way they are, and how humans can live in harmony with nature. To this day, when Aborigines die, they are recycled to the continuum of Dreamtime.

Discoveries

For hundreds of centuries the Aborigines had Australia to themselves. Over the last few hundred years, though, the rest of the world began closing in.

Like the search for El Dorado, everybody seemed to be looking for *Terra Australis Incognita* or "The Great Land of the South". On and off throughout the 16th century, explorers from Europe kept an eye peeled for the legendary continent and its presumed riches.

Some may have come close, but the first known landing was by a Dutch captain, Willem Jansz, in 1606. It was a bit of an

Lively figures illustrate Aboriginal legends in Kakadu.

anticlimax. "There was no good to be done there," was the conclusion as he weighed anchor.

Despite this letdown, the merchant adventurers of the Dutch East India Company, the developers of Java, Ceylon and the Cape of Good Hope, were not to be discouraged. In 1642 the company despatched one of its ace seafarers, Abel Tasman, to track down the elusive treasures of the furthest continent.

On his first expedition, Tasman discovered an island he called Van Diemen's Land; the modern name honours the finder: Tasmania. A couple of years later Tasman was sent back. He covered much of the coast of northern Australia, but still he found no gold, silver or spices. Like Jansz before him, Tasman had nothing good to say about the Aborigines, who impressed him as poor, hungry and generally unattractive brutes. The Dutch named Australia New Holland, but the reports were so unpromising that they never bothered to claim the land.

Another pessimistic view came from a colourful British traveller, the sometime swashbuckler William Dampier, who had two good looks at the west coast of Australia towards the end of the 17th century. He found no drinking water, no fruit or vegetables, no riches, and "the miserablest people in the world".

Botany Bay

Almost by accident, Captain James Cook, the great British navigator, landed on the east coast of Australia in 1770 on a very roundabout trip back to England from Tahiti. Aboard his ship *Endeavour* were two skilled naturalists, Joseph Banks and Daniel Solander. They found so many fascinating specimens that Cook was moved to name the place Botany Bay. (Later, *Endeavour* was holed by coral on a reef off Queensland; thus you could say Captain Cook discovered—the hard way—one of the natural wonders of the world, the Great Barrier Reef.)

Cook claimed all the territory he charted for King George III, coining the name New South Wales. He returned to London with glowing reports of the Australia he had glimpsed: a vast, sunny, fertile land, inhabited by Aborigines who were "far more happier than we Europeans". The captain's positive thinking about "noble savages" was to be the death of him. A few years later, on the island of Hawaii, he was slain and dismembered by a mob of angry Polynesians.

In 1779, Joseph Banks, by now the president of the Royal Academy, came up with a novel idea. He formally proposed colonizing Australia…but instead of the conventional type of settlers, he would send out convicts as pioneers. This plan, he contended, would solve the crisis in Britain's overflowing jails. The laws were severe in those days: even amateur criminals like petty larcenists, bigamists and army deserters faced exile.

For most of the 18th century, the British had disposed of troublesome convicts by banishing them to North America. With the American Revolution, though, this desirable destination had to be dropped from the itineraries. The motherland's prisons couldn't possibly cope, and the supplementary river hulks that were used as floating jails threatened riot and disease.

The Banks proposal for a British version of Devil's Island seemed far-fetched and expensive, but nobody had a better idea, and in May, 1787, His Majesty's Government began the transportation of criminals to Australia. The programme was to endure for 80 years. During that time more than 160,000 convicts were shipped out to a new life Down Under.

The First Fleet

A retired naval officer, Captain Arthur Phillip, was put in command of the first fleet of 11 sailing vessels carrying nearly 1,500 souls, more than half of them convicts, on an eight-month voyage from Portsmouth to New South Wales. Remarkably, the convoy was a total success.

Captain Phillip (now titled Governor), came ashore in full ceremonial dress but unarmed. Spear-toting natives milled about like an unwelcoming committee. A lieutenant on the flagship wrote: "I think it is very easy to conceive the ridiculous figure we must appear to these poor creatures, who were perfectly naked."

Unveiled, too, was the truth

Incredibilities

Who would believe that a creature as odd as the duckbill platypus has been living in Australia since the Ice Age? That so many explorers could come so close and yet miss discovering an island as big as Australia? That the first colonists would be jailbirds? That Captain Bligh, the Bounty tough guy, would be deposed for a second time, in Australia? That California miners would flock to Australia for a replay of the gold rush? That the national song—Waltzing Matilda—would glorify a tea-drinking sheep rustler? Who, indeed?

Mark Twain put it this way: "[Australian history] does not read like history but like the most beautiful lies... It is full of surprises, and adventures, and incongruities, and contradictions, and incredibilities; but they are all true; they all happened."

---

about Botany Bay: Captain Cook's rosy claims faded to bleak. The expedition's officers were appalled to discover that there was no shelter from east winds, that much of the alleged meadowland was actually swamp, and that there wasn't enough fresh water to go round.

Luckily, the next best thing to paradise was waiting just around the corner. Governor Phillip and a reconnaissance party sailed 12 miles up the coast and discovered what Fleet Surgeon John White called "the finest and most extensive harbour in the universe". It could, he reckoned, provide "safe anchorage for all the navies of Europe". It was also strikingly beautiful. Today it's called Sydney Harbour.

The fleet reassembled at Sydney Cove on January 26, 1788

(the date is recalled every year as the Australian national holiday), and the British flag was raised over the brand-new colony. A few Aborigines put on a noisy Aliens-Go-Home demonstration, but local opinion never discouraged an empire-builder.

Exuberantly painted, solemnly beribboned—two Australias honour sacred memories.

On Their Own

London's great expectations took it for granted that New South Wales would be instantly self-sufficient. Real life fell dangerously short of the theory. The Sydney summer was too hot for exertions. Even if the convicts had genuinely wanted to pitch in, the soil was unpromising. In any event, most of the outcasts were city-bred and couldn't tell the

difference between a hoe and a sickle. Livestock died or disappeared in the bush. Hunger crept into ambush.

Shipwrecks, and delays in London, meant that relief supplies were to be only a mirage for nearly two years of increasing desperation. As food supplies dwindled, rations were cut. Prisoners caught stealing food were flogged. Finally, to set an example, the governor ordered a food-looter executed.

In June, 1790, to all-round jubilation, the supply ship *Lady Juliana* reached Sydney harbour, and the long fast ended. As agriculture finally began to blossom, thousands of new prisoners were shipped out. And even voluntary settlers chose Australia as the land of their future.

Enter Captain Bligh

When Governor Phillip retired, the colony's top army officer, Major Francis Grose, took over. His army subordinates fared very well under the new regime, which encouraged free enterprise. The officers soon found profitable sidelines, usually at the expense of the British taxpayers. The army's monopoly on the sale of rum made quick fortunes; under some tipsy economic law, rum began to replace money as Australia's medium of exchange. Even prisoners were paid in alcohol for their extra-curricular jobs. Many hangovers ensued.

As news of widespread hanky-panky reached London, the government sent out a well-known disciplinarian to restore decorum in the colony. He was Captain William Bligh, target of the notorious mutiny on *H.M.S. Bounty* seven years earlier. Bligh meant to put fear into the hearts of backsliding officers, but his temper was beyond control. His

---

Fearless But Flawed

He might not have won any popularity contests, but revisionist historians say Captain Bligh really wasn't as bad as he's depicted.

Before his ill-fated career in Australia, Bligh achieved a courageous record. He sailed around the world with Captain Cook, served in naval battles, and showed superhuman survival instincts when the Bounty mutineers, preferring Tahiti to home, set him adrift in the Pacific. With fortitude, luck and exceptional navigating skill, he lived through a voyage of 3,600 miles in an open boat. By coincidence, Bligh was assigned to suppress a second naval mutiny, in 1797, before his appointment to shake up New South Wales.

The short-tempered captain, destined to be portrayed as one of Hollywood's most memorable villains, was eventually promoted to vice admiral.

New South Wales victims nicknamed the new governor Caligula and plotted treason.

Captain Bligh was deposed by a group of insurgent officers on January 26, 1808, as the colony toasted its 20th anniversary. The Rum Rebellion, as the mutiny was dubbed, led to a radical reorganization and reshuffle in personnel. But the inevitable courtmartial seemed to understand how Bligh's personality and methods had galled his subordinates. The mutineers were given more than a rap on the knuckles, but less than they might have expected.

Opening a Continent

Under Governor Lachlan Macquarie, New South Wales overcame the stigma of a penal colony and became a land of opportunity. The idealistic army officer built schools, a hospital, a courthouse, and roads to link them.

To inspire exiles to go straight and win emancipation, he appointed an ex-convict as Justice of the Peace, and he invited others to dinner, to the horror of the local élite. One of the criminals Macquarie pardoned, Francis Greenway, became the colony's prolific official architect.

Some ex-convicts fared so well under Macquarie's progressive policies that he was accused of pampering the criminal class.

London decreed tougher punishment, along with the total separation of prisoners from the rest of the population. All this led to long-lasting conflict between reformed criminals and their children on one side and a privileged class of immigrants on the other. Nowadays, the shoe is on the other foot: descendants of First Fleet prisoners often express the same kind of pride as Americans of *Mayflower* ancestry.

The biggest problem for Governor Macquarie and his immediate successors was the colony's position on the edge of the sea. There wasn't enough land to provide food for the expanding population. The Blue Mountains, which boxed in Sydney Cove, seemed a hopeless barrier. Every attempt to break through the labyrinth of steep valleys failed. Then in 1813, explorers Blaxland, Wentworth and Lawson had the unconventional idea of crossing the peaks rather than the vales. And it worked. On the far side of the Blue Mountains they discovered a land of plenty, endless plains that would support a great new society.

Other explorers—mostly surveyors, army men and eager colonists, with assistance from convicts and Aborigines—opened territories that were more distant but no less promising. Land was either confiscated or bought from the indigenous tribesmen: for 100,000 acres of what is now Melbourne the entrepreneurs gave the Aborigines a wagonload of clothing and blankets plus 30 knives, 12 tomahawks, 10 mirrors, 12 pairs of scissors and 50 pounds of flour. By the middle of the 19th century, thousands of settlers had poured into Australia, and all of the present state capitals were on the map.

Age of Gold

In his understandable enthusiasm, rancher Edward Hargraves slightly overstated the case when he declared: "This is a memorable day in the history of New South Wales. I shall be a baronet. You will be knighted, and my old horse will be stuffed, put in a glass case, and sent to the British Museum."

The date was 1851. The place was near Bathurst, about 130 miles west of Sydney. Hargraves' audience consisted of one speechless colleague. The occasion was the discovery of gold in Australia.

No sooner had the news of the Bathurst find reached the farthest corner of the continent than prospectors from Melbourne struck gold at Ballarat. With two colonies—New South Wales and

*In Western Australia,
a ghost town prospects for
new gold from tourism.*

OOLGARDIE
HOST MINING TOWN

CENTRAL COOLGARDIE

YOU ARE
HERE

FLY FLAT

TO KALGOORLIE

FROM SOUTHERN CROSS

LEFROY ST   HUNT ST

TO ESPERANCE

| HISTORY OF GOLD | TOWN POPULATION |

Victoria—sharing in the boom, adventurers streamed in from Europe and America. Among them were Australians who had tried to get rich in California's '49er stampede. By 1860 Australia's population had reached one million. Thirty-three years later the bonanza became a coast-to-coast celebration when gold was discovered in Kalgoorlie, Western Australia.

Life in the gold fields was rugged, aggravated by the climate, the flies and tax collectors. Whether big winners or, more likely, small losers, all the diggers had to pay the same licence fee. Enforcement and fines were needlessly strict. Justice, the miners felt, was tilted against them. They burned their licences and demonstrated for voting rights and other reforms. In the subsequent siege of the Eureka Stockade in Ballarat in 1854, troops were ordered to attack the demonstrators. There was heavy loss of life. The licence fee was abandoned.

Another riot, in 1861, pitted the white prospectors against Chinese miners, who were resented for their foreignness, for working too hard and spending too little. At Lambing Flat, New South Wales, thousands of whites whipped and clubbed a community of Chinese. Police, troops and finally the courts dealt leniently with the attackers. It was the worst of several race riots. With the tensions of the gold rush, the notion of the yellow peril was embedded in Australia's national consciousness.

Rogues on the Range

Transportation of convicts finally ended in 1868, when London had to admit that the threat of exile in golden Australia was no deterrent to crime.

In Australia itself, crime was always something of a problem; nobody really expected every last sinner to go straight as soon as he arrived. Some wily characters, often escaped convicts, became bushrangers, the local version of highwaymen. They occasionally attracted sympathy from Outback folk because they tended to rob the rich and flout authority. As the crimes grew more ambitious or outrageous, their fame was frozen into legend.

The saga of Ned Kelly (1854–1880) reads like Robin Hood gone sour. The Kelly gang preyed on bankers rather than humble ranchers, and Kelly's imaginative operations could be spectacular. But he killed more than his quota of policemen, almost for the fun of it. Wounded in a shootout, Kelly tried to escape in a suit of homemade armour; this nightmarish contraption deflected most of the bullets, and he was captured wounded but alive. Sentenced to death, he cheekily invited the judge to meet him in the hereafter. Two weeks after Kelly was hanged, the judge, indeed, died.

The New Century
With the blessing of Queen Victoria, the colonies of Australia formed a new nation, the Commonwealth of Australia, on New Year's Day, 1901. This federation retained the Queen as head of state, and bowed as well to the parliament and privy council in London.

Loyalty to the British Empire was tested twice, extravagantly, in the world wars. The Allied defeat at Gallipoli in 1915 was the first and the most memorable single disaster for the gallant "diggers". By the end of World War I, more than 200,000 Australians—two-thirds of the entire expeditionary force—had been killed or wounded.

The combat came closer in World War II, when Japanese planes repeatedly bombed Darwin, enemy submarines penetrated Sydney harbour, and invasion became a real threat. The statistics: 27,000 Australian servicemen died in action on the European and Asian fronts, and nearly 8,000 more died as prisoners of Japan.

Ned Kelly—a rogue remembered with humour and affection—lives on in Melbourne Gaol.

HISTORY

Postwar Australia was a different place, feeling itself part of Asia, vulnerable, and dependent on the United States rather than Britain. ANZUS, a defensive alliance of Australia, New Zealand and the United States, was founded in 1951. Australian land, air and sea forces—40 per cent of them conscripts—fought alongside the Americans in Vietnam, an involvement that lasted from 1965 until 1972.

The tilt towards Asia and America showed up no less in the trade balance. Before World War II, 42 per cent of Australia's overseas trade was with Britain. In recent times, the entire European Community is down to second or third place in the commercial charts, behind the U.S. or Japan or both.

Another obvious change in orientation is the racial and national background of Australians. Before World War II, 98 per cent of the population was British born or of British descent. After the war, throngs of Greeks, Yugoslavs, Italians and northern Europeans settled in Australia; more than 10 per cent of immigrants were refugees or displaced persons. The fortress walls of the "White Australia" immigration policy, enacted in 1901 to maintain racial purity, stood firm for well over half a century. But now the Asian presence has begun to reflect the

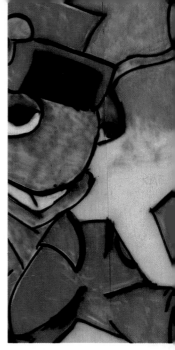

strength of trade ties with Australia's neighbours.

Policy towards the Aborigines softened as well. As recently as 1960, Australia's first settlers were granted citizenship and social service benefits. While the Aborigines struggled for land rights, the government intensified efforts to overcome their disadvantages in health, wealth and education.

In the usual cut and thrust of

Political graffiti and fantasy art add colour to Sydney quayside.

politics, prime ministers of right and left came and went, but two of them departed dramatically. In 1967 Harold Holt vanished while swimming off the coast of Victoria. In 1975, in a profound constitutional crisis, Gough Whitlam was deposed by the governor-general.

In the 1980s, international and domestic economic difficulties darkened the abiding Australian dream of boundless prosperity. Tightened belts had been out of fashion since hunger gnawed at the First Fleet, but the government turned to austerity measures to ride out the crisis. In spite of all the problems, Australia staked its sunshine and friendly charm on a snowballing success in international tourism.

33

HISTORICAL LANDMARKS

Dreamtime	40,000 B.C.	Aboriginal people, Stone Age migrants from Asia, inhabit the Australian continent, developing traditions of a society that survives by hunting, fishing and gathering food.
Discoveries	c.1600 A.D.	European explorers sight long-sought *Terra Australis Incognita* but are unimpressed.
	1606	Willem Jansz makes first known landing.
	1642	Dutch navigator Abel Tasman discovers and names Van Diemen's Land (Tasmania) and Statenland (New Zealand).
Settlement	1770	Captain James Cook explores east coast of Australia, names it New South Wales and claims it for King George III.
	1788	British penal colony established at Sydney Cove.
	1793	Free settlers begin to arrive. Estimated Aboriginal population of 300,000 forced to make way for colonists.
	1808	Rum Rebellion overthrows the governor, Captain William Bligh.
	1813	Blaxland, Wentworth and Lawson cross the Blue Mountains.
	1823	John Oxley discovers the Brisbane River; two years later Brisbane is founded.
	1828	In the first census, 36,000 free settlers and convicts are counted.

Age of Gold	1851	Edward Hargraves discovers gold in New South Wales.
	1854	Eureka riot in Ballarat.
	1860	Population attains 1 million.
	1861	Anti-Chinese riots in gold fields.
	1868	British government ends transportation of convicts to Australia.
	1899	Australian troops sent to South Africa to fight in Boer War.
The New Century	1901	Commonwealth of Australia proclaimed on New Year's Day.
	1908	Canberra chosen as site for a new federal capital.
	1911	Canberra designed by American architect Burley Griffin, and construction begins.
	1914–18	Australia joins Allies in World War I, suffering considerable losses at Gallipoli and in France.
	1917	Transcontinental railway opened.
	1920	First airline service opened.
	1927	Seat of government is moved from Melbourne to Canberra.
	1942–45	In World War II Japanese bomb Darwin, threaten invasion; Australian forces count 35,000 dead.
	1953	British atomic weapons tested in South Australian desert.
	1960	Australia grants citizenship to Aborigines; two years later they obtain the right to vote.
	1965	Australian troops sent to fight in Vietnam war.
	1972	"White Australia" immigration policy abandoned.

WHERE TO GO

Deciding where to go and what to see in Australia may be the hardest part of the journey. How to cram in so much in a limited time?

Although air fares are expensive, about 11 million passengers a year fly the domestic airline routes. Overseas tourists can benefit from solid discounts on internal flights, providing they plan ahead. The alternatives are slower but often more revealing: transcontinental trains and long-distance buses, some equipped for luxury travel.

Since you probably can't see all of it, you'll have to arrange your tour of Australia to concentrate on a manageable slice or two. Planning your itinerary requires a compromise involving the time and funds available, the season, your special interests, and your choice of gateway city. But why not arrive in, say, Sydney and depart from Perth? Or in at Darwin, for instance, and out at Melbourne?

This section of our travel guide is arranged according to the geographic reality of Australia's states. Although there is no visible difference between the red deserts of the Northern Territory or those of South Australia, it's convenient to consider them in the context of the political frontiers. Besides, the way history and chance carved Australia into states comes fairly close to a manageable division into sightseeing regions.

In each state we start with the capital city gateway and fan out from there. We begin where Australia itself began, at Sydney Cove. After a side trip to the federal capital, Canberra, we continue beyond New South Wales, in an anticlockwise direction, from Brisbane in Queensland to Melbourne in Victoria. Our Where to Go section winds up with the continent's lovely green footnote, Tasmania.

The endless beaches are irresistible—and you don't have to go far to find them.

NEW SOUTH WALES

Sydney can't help but dominate New South Wales, if only because most of the state's population lives in the capital. But beyond the metropolis, the state—six times the size of England—is as varied as dairyland and desert, as vineyards and craggy mountains.

SYDNEY

Ever since 1788, when the first convoy of convicts arrived to build a new nation, Sydney's harbour has stolen the show. It is so stunning that people alongside are inspired to achievement and *joie de vivre*.

Australia's oldest, liveliest and biggest city (population 3½ million) has good reason for self-satisfaction. A typically chauvinistic slogan of the 1980s thumbed the city's nose at the rest of Australia and, for that matter, the world: "If you're not living in Sydney, you're camping out."

Brawny and brazen, Sydney is a sophisticated financial, communications and manufacturing centre. After hours—and Sydneysiders live for the after hours—there is every imaginable cosmopolitan delight. And it's a sunny coincidence that beaches famous for surfing and scenery are only a few minutes away.

Most of the world's great cities have a landmark that serves as an instantly recognizable symbol. Sydney has two: the perfect arch of the Harbour Bridge and the billowing roofs of the Opera House. That's what happens when engineers and architects embellish a harbour coveted by artists as well as admirals.

City Sights

For a quick appreciation of the intricacies of **Port Jackson** (the official name for Sydney harbour), gaze down from the top of Sydney's tallest building or take a helicopter tour. See the clear blue tentacles of water stretching from the South Pacific into the heart of the city. Schools of sailing boats vaunt the harbour's perfection in the reflection of the skyscrapers, the classic bridge and the exhilarating opera house. A pity Captain Cook never noticed this glorious setting as he sailed right past on his way home from Botany Bay.

Most sightseeing tours—by land or sea—leave from **Circular Quay** (short for *Semi*-Circular Quay, as it was more accurately named in olden times). Cruise ships and water taxis alike tie up here, but most of the action involves commuter ferryboats and hydrofoils. The quayside's quota of human interest features hasty travellers, leisurely sightseers, street musicians, artists and hawkers. Whether you see Australia's busiest harbour from the deck of a luxury liner, a sightseeing boat or a humble ferry, don't miss this invigorating angle on the city's skyline.

The Rocks

To start at the beginning, stroll through the charming streets of The Rocks, the neighbourhood where Sydney was born. Here modern Australia's founding fathers—convicts charged with anything from murder to shoplifting—came ashore in 1788 to build the colony of New South Wales. Recently restored and revivified, this historic waterfront district has everything a tourist could want: lovely views at long and short range, moody old buildings, cheerful plazas, and plenty of distractions in the way of shopping, eating and drinking.

Pick up local leaflets and maps at **The Rocks Visitors' Centre,** 104 George Street. This building,

too, has a bit of a history. It was built in 1907 as the Coroner's Court. That, you'll be relieved to know, is why the doors to the rest rooms are marked "Male Witnesses" and "Female Witnesses".

Cadman's Cottage, next door, is Sydney's oldest (1816) surviving house—a simple stone cottage long occupied by the government's boatmen. It's now a small maritime museum, with anchors, sails, oars and the like.

Campbell's Storehouse, farther along the cove, is a venerable warehouse converted into an attractive complex of shops, restaurants and a wine bar for connoisseurs. Another commercial highlight in a former warehouse, **Argyle Arts Centre** now houses restaurants, arts and crafts shops and galleries.

Argyle Cut, a shady underpass, indicates why the first generation of convicts named this district The Rocks. To excavate this route, work parties were ordered to chop through solid rock with pickaxes. It took them years. The topless tunnel was later widened by mechanical means. In Sydney's boisterous 19th century, this was the likeliest place in town to get mugged.

High above The Rocks, **Observatory Hill** is a fine spot to observe the heavens, or the heavenly prospect of Sydney harbour.

> ### The "Coathanger" Incident
>
> *When the Sydney Harbour Bridge, nicknamed "The Coathanger", was officially opened on March 19, 1932, the crowd witnessed an unscheduled spectacle.*
>
> *As the premier of New South Wales prepared to wield his ceremonial scissors, a figure on horseback, dressed in an old British army uniform, galloped up and slashed the symbolic ribbon with a sabre. The intruder was Francis de Groot, leader of a right-wing organization representing what he called "the decent citizens", as opposed to the socialist government of the state. The scene-stealing fanatic was bundled off the bridge and later fined £4 for offensive behaviour. The ribbon was retied and, anticlimactically, snipped with official pomp.*
>
> *Before the day was over, about 300,000 people really made it official: they hiked across the bridge.*

Since the middle of the 19th century, at precisely 1 p.m. every day, a ball has been dropped from a mast here for ship's captains to set their chronometers.

Clumps of terrace houses on the **Millers Point** side of the peninsula are preserved as architectural monuments. So are a couple of the oldest **pubs** in Australia, redolent of history as well as beer. If you need an excuse, the Hero of Waterloo in Lower Fort Street and the Lord Nelson Hotel near Argyle Place are worth visiting for scholarly purposes. Back on the waterfront, **Pier One** is an old multistorey shipping terminal now done up as a big shopping and leisure centre.

From the grassy hillside of **Dawes Point Park**, studded with old cannon, you can survey the harbour's froth of ferries, hydrofoils and sailing boats. On a

warm day you'll appreciate the shade of the trees and the bridge-work directly above. This is not just any old bridge. With its drive-through stone pillars and geometrically impeccable steel arch, the **Sydney Harbour Bridge** strides confidently across the harbour, adding to the fascination of an already splendid scene.

Linking the city and the north, the bridge's single arch is 503 metres (1,650 feet) across, and

Pages 40–41: Golden glints on Sydney Harbour Bridge. Above: A century of architecture.

wide enough to carry eight lanes of cars, two railway tracks, and lanes for pedestrians and cyclists. When it was built, during the Great Depression, Sydneysiders called the bridge the Iron Lung, because it kept a lot of people "breathing"—in economic terms. It remains a

source of employment, for instance for tollkeepers and daredevil painters. It takes ten years to repaint the bridge, and then it's time to start again.

An unusual vantage point for viewing the bridge, the harbour and skyline is from the top of one of the bridge's massive pylons. The **lookout** is in the south-east tower, and the stairway can be reached via Cumberland Street, The Rocks. It's open only on Saturdays, Sundays, Mondays and legal holidays.

City Centre

Open every day of the year except Christmas, the **Sydney Tower** at Centrepoint is the skyscraper city's highest vantage point—305 metres (1,000 feet) above the street. It takes only 40 seconds to whoosh straight up to the observation decks (and the revolving restaurants travellers can hardly avoid at such altitudes). Amateur photographers get that glazed look as they peer hungrily through the tinted windows to unlimited horizons. Thoughtfully, the management also installed some *un*tinted glass so that cameras can capture authentic colours. On a flawless day you can see all the way to Terrigal and Wollongong,

Round-up of Sydneysiders enjoying a sunny break in Martin Place.

45

far out to sea or to the Blue Mountains. Otherwise, look out and down at the seething shopping streets all around the tower.

Most Australian cities and towns now have pedestrian malls, normally the heart of the downtown shopping district, lined with department stores and fashionable boutiques. Sydney has a different sort of mall: **Martin Place** is a wide, car-less street of trees and fountains, just for strolling, meeting friends, and breathing some non-aircondi-tioned air. While you're here, you can mail your postcards from the vast Victorian Renaissance building of the **General Post Office.** During World War II the GPO's landmark clock tower was dismantled—not because the correct time was a military secret, but as a precaution in case the enemy tried to knock it off.

From the same era as the GPO, but even grander, the **Queen Victoria Building** occupies an entire block on George Street, Sydney's main street (and the oldest street in the country). Its fine stonework and interior details have been restored to the old elegance as a multipurpose tourist and shopping centre.

Next door, Sydney's **Town Hall** enlivens a site that used to be a cemetery. The overblown Victorian building, home of the city council, is also used for concerts and exhibitions.

Chinatown

After dark, Sydney doesn't re-treat to the suburbs the way most Australian cities do. One centre of nocturnal attraction, along George Street heading south from the Town Hall, is a row of first-run cinemas. In the adjacent Chinatown district, gourmets can abandon them-selves to the delights of Peking, Cantonese or Szechuan cuisine. The local Chinese community (estimated at about 60,000) is joined by enthusiastic Sydney-siders and tourists enjoying the choice of Chinese cafés and res-taurants, and shops selling exotic spices and knick-knacks. The district's centrepiece is **Dixon Street,** a pedestrian zone framed by ceremonial wooden gates and illuminated by distinctive lamps.

The **Sydney Entertainment Centre,** on the western flank of Chinatown, was designed to be used for sports events, concerts and almost any other public event. A full house here amounts to 12,500 spectators.

If you're in the neighbourhood over the weekend, check out **Paddy's Market,** a cavernous brick building full of stalls selling almost anything: souvenirs,

On the brink of Chinatown, pink brick arches lead to Paddy's Market.

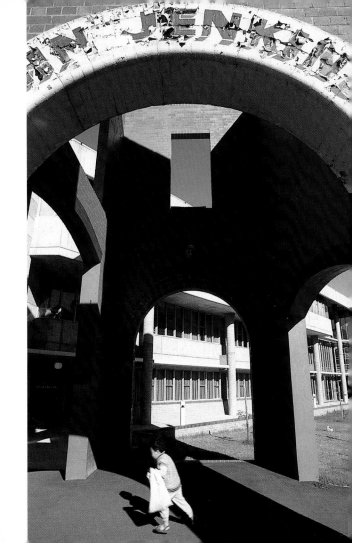

seashells, sunglasses and semi-antiques. In the fruit and vegetable department the salesmen keep up a stream of entertaining chatter and come-ons.

The Parks

All cities should have parks in the middle; Sydney has its share. Although **Hyde Park** is only a fraction the size of its namesake in London, it provides the same sort of green relief. The most formal feature of these semi-formal gardens, the **Anzac War Memorial**, commemorates the World War I fighters in monumental Art Deco style.

Sightseers who collect old churches should mark three targets on the edge of Hyde Park. To the north, the early colonial **St. James' Church** in Queens Square was the work of the convict architect, Francis Greenway. Across College Street on the east, **St. Mary's Cathedral** stands on the prominent site of the colony's first Catholic church. Its Gothic-style spires were designed in the second half of the 19th century. From the same era, the **Great Synagogue** faces the park across Elizabeth Street. Jews have lived in Sydney since the arrival of the first shipment of prisoners.

The **Australian Museum**, on College Street, specializes in natural history and anthropology. There are fossils, dinosaurs and stuffed birds—the sort of things children are dragged to museums to be shown. The museum also has a good section on the art, culture and recent history of the Aborigines. While you're there, browse through the Aboriginal arts and crafts on sale in the big Museum Shop.

Children are well catered for in the restored **Hyde Park Bar-**

Emancipated Architecture

If Sydney had been ready for an opera house in 1820, Francis Greenway would have built it.

Under dynamic Governor Lachlan Macquarie, Greenway designed everything from churches to barracks to a lighthouse. A bankrupt architect in England, Greenway had been convicted of forging a clause in a building contract. In 1812 this crime carried the death penalty, but he was lucky enough to have it commuted to 14 years of exile in Australia.

Making the best of a seemingly grim future, Greenway soon won parole and, as the only competent builder in town, stepped into the job of government architect. His projects for Sydney grew ever grander, to the delight of the governor. But the rulers in London finally complained that extravagance was no way to build a penal colony. Greenway was fired in 1822, but his monuments are all around you in the city he built.

---

racks (designed by Greenway), now a museum of social history, between the park and the Botanic Gardens. On the top floor of the barracks, one large room is a reconstruction of the dormitory life of the prisoners. The present keepers don't seem to mind when youngsters can't resist testing the hammocks. **The Mint**, next door, has exhibits on money, stamps, flags and other acute angles on Australian history.

For a century or so, the park called **The Domain** has contained the local equivalent of London's Hyde Park Corner, where anyone can climb aboard a soapbox and make a speech; Sunday is the day of the orators and hecklers. The **Art Gallery of New South Wales** consists of an old and new building attached like ill-matched Siamese twins. Nineteenth- and twentieth-century art is surveyed here, along with a concise review of Aboriginal art and an enviable collection of the sculptures and masks of South Pacific islanders.

Sydney's **Royal Botanic Gardens** began as a different sort of garden: here the early colonists first tried—with very limited success—to grow vegetables. Only a few steps from the busy skyscraper world of downtown Sydney, you can relax in the shade of Moreton Bay fig trees, palms or mighty mahoganies, or enter a glass pyramid full of

orchids and other tropical beauties. The gardens curve up around Farm Cove to a peninsula with the quaint name of **Mrs. Macquarie's Point**. The lady thus immortalized, the wife of the go-ahead governor, used to admire the view from here; now it's better than ever.

Sydney Opera House

Australians are notoriously casual, but there's a real sense of occasion about the Sydney Opera House, both inside and out. This one-in-a-million building, covered in a million tiles, has brought glory to the city, the country, and the controversial architect who left in a huff at an early stage of construction.

Until the opera house idea caught on, the promontory was wasted on a fancy, turreted depot for tramcars. At the end of the line, Bennelong Point was hardly a site for sore eyes. In the 1950s the government of New South Wales decided to build a performing arts centre there. A Danish architect, Jørn Utzon, won an international competition to design it. His novel plan included problems of spherical geometry so tricky that he actually chopped up a wooden sphere to prove it could be done.

The inspiring shell of the complex was virtually complete when Utzon walked out; the interior, which was in dispute, became the work of a committee. Even so, from the tip of its highest roof (67 metres [221 feet] above sea level), to the Drama Theatre's orchestra pit (more than a fathom *below* sea level) this place has grace, taste and class.

The name "Sydney Opera House" is as renowned as it is inaccurate. The actual opera theatre is only one of the centre's five, and not the biggest. (Inci-

dentally, if you're "fashionably late" for the opera, there's no admission until the first break, probably the end of the first act —and that goes for VIPs as well as tourists.) It's well worth taking one of the guided tours around the premises.

The roofs of Sydney's Opera House: a stunning sight from any angle.

Kings Cross

East of the Domain lies the district of Woolloomooloo (the nifty name has something to do with kangaroos in an Aboriginal language). And east of Woolloomooloo looms loose-moraled Kings Cross, the Sydney version of Paris's Pigalle or London's Soho. Kings Cross first came to international attention in the 1960s when United States troops, flown over from Vietnam for brief spells of respite from war, discovered its potential for "R & R"—"rest and recreation". Mostly recreation.

Everything is for sale in The Cross. Doormen representing the fleshpots importune almost all the passers-by, and so, less pushily, do hordes of streetwalkers. There's nothing quite like it elsewhere in Australia.

But the gaudy nightlife district has more to offer than sin. There are reputable hotels and shops, a very original fountain commem-

$100 Million Overrun

These big projects always cost more than you think. Sydney's Opera House was first budgeted for $7 million. By the time it was finished 19 years later, $102 million turned out to be closer to the mark. To make up the difference, culture-lovers and others bought "Opera House" lottery tickets that more than paid the bill.

Some other statistics:

The ingenious billowing roofs weigh 160,965 tonnes.

The roofs' 1,056,000 ceramic tiles, made in Sweden, wash themselves when it rains.

There are 6,223 square metres (66,985 square feet) of glass, made in France.

There are five theatres, an exhibition hall, two restaurants and six bars.

orating the World War II desert battle of El Alamein, and some good ethnic restaurants.

A five-minute walk from Kings Cross Station, **Elizabeth Bay House** is a stately home built in 1835, now restored and open for inspection (but never on Mondays). The centre of architectural interest is an ingenious elliptical staircase, suitable for the most dramatic entrance. The upper floor offers a gorgeous view of the eastern reaches of the harbour.

If you have time for one more inner suburb, make it **Paddington**, south-east of Kings Cross. Its trademark is the intricate wrought-ironwork, known as Sydney Lace, on the balconies of 19th-century terraced houses. This feature, and the rather bohemian atmosphere, reminds some travellers of New Orleans. After decades of dilapidation, the district has come up in the world as a fashionable, rather arty place to live. "Paddo", as the locals like to call it, is full of far-out ethnic restaurants, antique shops, art galleries and trendy boutiques.

Around Sydney Harbour

Unless you take a cruise around the harbour you'll never appreciate its unexpectedly varied ins and outs: the hidden beaches, islets, mansions old and new, even a couple of unsung bridges.

Various firms run half-day and full-day excursions. Or you can hire a boat of your own and weave around the nautical traffic.

Among the harbour highlights:

Fort Denison occupies a small island graphically nicknamed "Pinchgut": before the construction of a proper prison, the colony's troublesome convicts were banished to the rock with a bread-and-water diet. In the middle of the 19th century it was fortified to guard Sydney from the far-fetched threat of a Russian attack. But the only attack came in World War II when an American warship, conducting target practice, hit old Pinchgut by mistake.

Taronga Zoo, a 12-minute ferry ride from Circular Quay, is not one of the world's greatest zoos, but you can't beat the setting. Over the heads of the giraffes you can see across the harbour to the skyscrapers of Sydney. Taronga Zoo claims a particularly chirpy collection of 1,500 Australian birds of about 200 species. As for the indigenous animals, the best time to see the koalas is around 3 p.m.,

Through a glass, brightly, patrons of a bar in the Rocks raise a cheery toast.

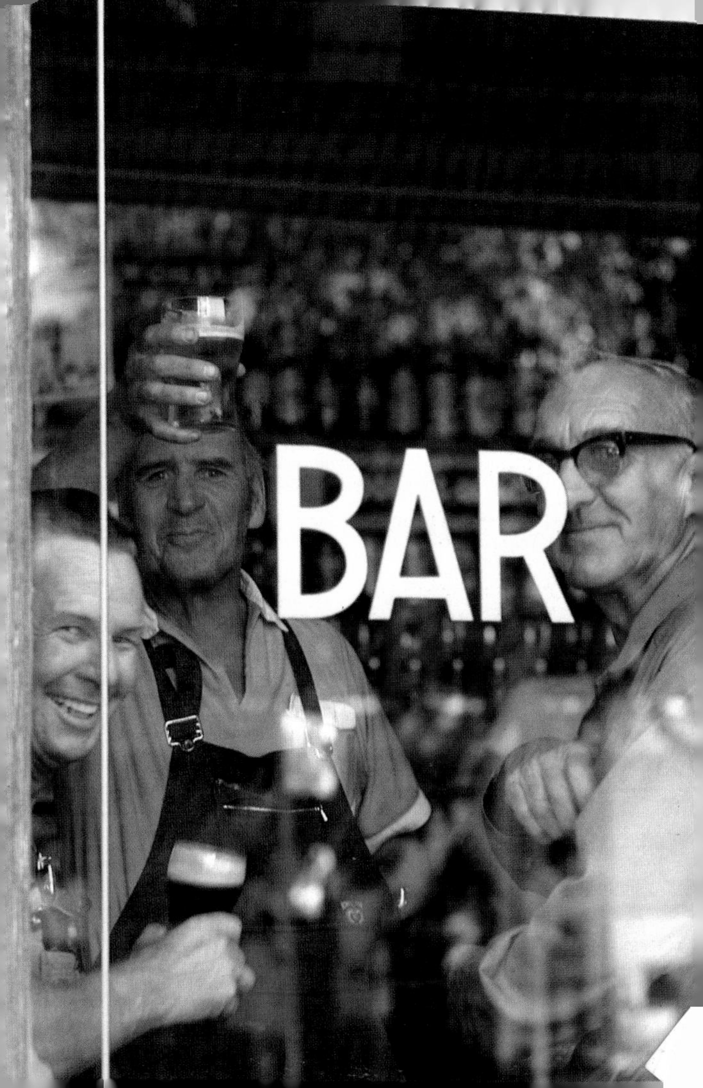
BAR

when they deign to awaken for feeding time. The best hours for platypuses: 11 a.m. to noon and 2 to 3 p.m.

Shark Island—popular with picnickers—is no more prone to fishy perils than any other place in the harbour; its shape, though, may have reminded people of a shark. Until anti-shark nets were installed at Sydney beaches in the 1930s, Australia could boast the world's highest incidence of shark attacks.

Vaucluse House, a stately home with its own beach, adds its mock-Gothic turrets and battlements to the skyline. The 15-room mansion, begun in 1803, is now run by the state's Historic Houses Trust. It's also reachable by bus or taxi.

Farther afield, both north and south of Sydney, are miles of inviting beaches. **Manly** got its

Sydney pastimes: sailing before the wind; a happy paddle.

name, we're told, because the first governor of the colony thought the Aborigines sunning themselves on the beach looked manly. This pleasant north shore resort has beaches back to back, linked by the lively Corso—a promenade full of restaurants and tables for picnickers. To defend local modesty, daylight bathing was forbidden in Manly until 1903. **Bondi**, pronounced *bond-eye,* is a favourite with surfers. The varied cast of characters on the sand ranges from ancient sunworshippers to bathing beauties and includes a statistically improbable crowd of New Zealanders. If a warning bell clangs, it signifies a shark alert; perhaps a false alarm, but it doesn't hurt to err on the cautious side.

Finally, back to the beginning at **Botany Bay,** where the colony of New South Wales was almost founded. This particular historic site is bypassed by the excursion buses; nor do public buses or trains go to Botany Bay, though the airliners descend over it on the final approach to Sydney's Kingsford Smith airport at Mascot. A monument and a museum commemorate the landing place of Captain Cook and his eager botanists in 1770.

Those Lifesavers

Australians didn't get a taste for surf bathing until the beginning of the 20th century. Only a wave or two behind them, the first lifeguards plunged in.

Dating back to 1907, the New South Wales Surf Bathing Association was the founding great-grandfather of all those bronzed lifeguards in colourful bathing caps guarding the beaches. Australia's glamorous sentinels of the coastline have rescued hundreds of thousands of swimmers.

Armed with rope reels or rescue boards and boats, the highly trained lifesavers are a reassuring part of the seaside scenery. Two things have changed in recent times: professional lifeguards now work alongside the volunteers; and women are welcome in the corps.

EXCURSIONS

Within day-trip distance of Sydney—by car, train or sightseeing bus—a choice of scene-changers shows the big variety of attractions offered by New South Wales. Any of the most popular outings will deepen your understanding of Australia and its assets.

Blue Mountains

Upon reflection, the brilliant idea seems obvious. The Blue Mountains, rugged enough to have cramped the young colony of New South Wales into a corner of the continent, weren't really insurmountable. Only the valleys were impassable—deep gorges like a Grand Canyon filled with eucalyptus forests. In 1813 a party of explorers finally conquered the Great Dividing Range by crossing the summits.

What a thrill the first over-the-top travellers must have felt when they spied the western plains beyond the "impenetrable" Blue Mountains. The blueness, incidentally, is explained by the refraction of light through the haze of eucalyptus oil evaporating from the billions of leaves.

The region's tourist centre, the historic town of **Katoomba,** looks out on a famous rock formation, the **Three Sisters.** This is the kind of sculptured outcrop that is bound to be surrounded by legend. The three sisters were turned into stone by their witch doctor father, to save them from the jaws of the dreaded "bunyip" whom they accidentally awoke. The father changed himself into a lyrebird and hid in a little cave, but lost his magic bone in the process. He is still looking for it today, and while the three sisters watch and wait on their mountain ledge, you can hear the call of Tyawan the lyrebird echoing through the valley.

Everywhere there are basalt and sandstone cliffs to please the most discerning mountain-climber. Exciting perspectives on all this are offered from the Scenic Railway, claiming to be the world's steepest railway line, and the Scenic Skyway, an aerial cable car.

For more than a century, spelunkers and ordinary tourists have admired the **Jenolan Caves**, at the end of a long, steep drive down the mountains from Katoomba. Guided tours through the spooky but often awesome limestone caverns last about an hour and a half. The atmosphere is cool in summer, warm in winter, and always damp.

Old Sydney Town

North of Sydney, beyond the sparkling waters of the Hawkesbury River, history buffs can visit a reconstruction of the original penal colony, Old Sydney Town. Here budding actors in period costumes duel, march, fire musket and cannon, and generally keep busy to amuse and inform visitors. A blacksmith, a potter and a candlestick-maker work at their traditional crafts, and a "magistrate" shows how summary justice used to be dealt.

On the way to Old Sydney Town, the Pacific Highway cuts through **Ku-ring-gai Chase National Park.** This compact area of unspoiled forests, cliffs and heathland is home base for numerous species of animals and birds. But you have to find them for yourself; it's not a zoo. By way of man-made attractions, the Aborigines who lived in this area long before the foundation of New South Wales left hundreds of rock carvings—pictures of animals and supernatural beings. The park information centre has maps pinpointing the location of the most interesting carvings.

Hunter Valley

Australia produces only about 1 per cent of all the world's wine, but that's more than enough to keep the country in good spirits; the overspill is exported. In the Hunter Valley, one of the nation's principal wine regions, they take their wines, from rieslings to madeiras, very seriously. The scenery of rolling hills is always attractive, the more so when the vines are ar-

57

rayed on a slope with forested mountains as the backdrop.

The Hunter Valley's main town, **Cessnock,** 195 kilometres (120 miles) north of Sydney, is surrounded by about 30 wineries. Many of these establishments are open for wine tastings, which can be jammed with enthusiasts on Sundays and holidays. To discourage the flightier sort of visitors, who tend to down the samples in undiscerning haste, most of the wineries now charge an entry fee. But you're under no obligation to buy a bottle of the local speciality or any of the other souvenirs on sale.

Although the romance of the grape accounts for the popularity of the Hunter Valley, the region is also industrial, with several huge power stations. Near the coal-mining and ship-building centre of Newcastle, the salt waters of **Lake Macquarie** attract weekend sailors and fishermen. It's said to be the largest seaboard lake in Australia.

Lord Howe Island
In the South Pacific, 483 kilometres (300 miles) east of Port Macquarie, Lord Howe Island, the state's off-shore possession, is said to be the world's most southerly coral isle. This makes

Troubadour brings history to life for Old Sydney Town visitors.

for splendid snorkelling and scuba diving... or you can go out to the sea gardens in a glass-bottomed boat. Forests, beaches, mountains and all, Lord Howe Island only amounts to a speck in the ocean—1,305 hectares (3,225 acres)—so bicycles and motorbikes are ideal for getting around.

You can fly out from Sydney to this sleepy lagoon in a couple of hours.

SNOWY MOUNTAINS
If you've come to Australia in search of snow, go no further than the south-eastern corner of New South Wales. Skiing in the Snowy Mountains is usually restricted to July, August and September. But even in the summer a few drifts of snow remain to frame the wild flowers of the Australian Alps. The top of this world is Mount Kosciusko, 2,228 metres (7,316 feet) high, named after an 18th-century Polish patriot by a 19th-century Polish explorer. This is the birthplace of three important rivers, the Murray, Murrumbidgee and Snowy. **Kosciusko National Park** is about 6,300 square kilometres (2,450 square miles) of the kind of wilderness you won't see anywhere else: buttercups and eucalyptus and snow, all in the same panorama. The only thing missing is a pine tree, or any of

59

the other familiar conifers of the northern hemisphere. Cars must be fitted with snow chains from June 1 to October 10. But even in summer the weather can change for the worse, and you should carry a warm, waterproof jacket. The best known ski resorts are **Thredbo** and **Perisher Valley.**

More sheep than men in the Australian Outback.

N.S.W. OUTBACK

Although New South Wales is the most populous and productive state (in both manufacturing and farming), it extends to infinities of real Australian Outback ... bushland and cattle stations that seem far more than a thousand miles from commuterland.

Gulgong once called itself the Athens of the West, but that was in the gold rush days when the

footlights were up at the Prince of Wales Opera House. The local Pioneer Museum reflects most aspects of frontier life with invaluable artefacts. This is the town where the bush poet Henry Lawson grew up; he and Gulgong are depicted on the back of the Australian $10 note.

Dubbo is the sort of place where the Old Gaol (jail), meticulously restored, is a prime tour-

ist attraction, gallows and all. Just out of town, the Western Plains Zoo is advertised as Australia's only open-range zoo, a cageless convention of koalas, dingoes and emus, plus more exotic (to Australians) animals like giraffes, zebras and monkeys.

Lightning Ridge, in the Back of Beyond near the Queensland border, enjoys one of the most evocative Outback names. For-

tune-hunters know it well as the home—reputedly the only home —of the precious black opal. Tourists are treated to demonstrations of fossicking, and there are opportunities to shop for opals.

Bourke is a small town whose very name signifies the loneliness of the Outback, where dusty tracks are the only link between distant hamlets. "Back of Bourke" is an Australian expression for *really* far-out Outback. Bourke looks a lot bigger on the map than on the ground.

Broken Hill (population more than 25,000) is about as far west as you can go in New South Wales, almost on the border of South Australia. The town is legendary for its mineral wealth —millions of tons of silver, lead and zinc. Tourists can visit the mines, which are either underground or on the top. And the neatly laid out town, its streets named after minerals—Iodide, Kaolin, Talc—is something of an artistic centre, as well, with Outback painters on show in a gaggle of local galleries.

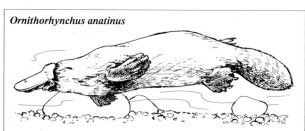

Ornithorhynchus anatinus

That's the Latin name for a creature so bizarre that the first eyewitness reports were dismissed as a hoax. But it's true: the platypus, an Australian exclusive, combines characteristics of mammal, reptile and bird. With its duck's bill, furry body, webbed feet and long tail, the amphibious platypus looks as unlikely as a winged pig.

The female platypus is notable as a mammal which lays eggs—one to three a year, with a leathery skin rather than a shell. The male is distinguished by the menacing spur on its hind leg, containing a poison gland. This is one of the reasons a platypus, which only grows to about 60 centimetres (2 feet), would make a less-than-perfect house pet.

The platypus's weird but sensitive bill is useful for smelling out food, both in and out of the water.

CANBERRA

Australia, the lucky country, lived up to its reputation when it came to picking the site for a national capital. Out of conflict emerged a green and pleasant compromise, far from the pressures of the big cities. Where sheep had grazed, the young Commonwealth raised its flag.

When the new nation was proclaimed at the turn of the 20th century, the perennial power struggle between Sydney and Melbourne reached an awkward deadlock. Each of the cities offset its rival's claim to be the national capital. So they carved out a site in the rolling bush 320 kilometres (200 miles) south-west of Sydney, and soon it began to sprout clean white official buildings, followed by millions of trees and shrubs. As compromises go, it was a winner.

To design a model capital from scratch, the way Washington, D.C., or St. Petersburg, U.S.S.R., were laid out, Australia opened an international competition. The prize went to an American architect, Walter Burley Griffin. He did, indeed, have a grand design. But it took longer than anyone imagined to transfer his plan from the drawing board to reality, owing to the distractions of two world wars, the depression, and a great deal of wrangling. Burley Griffin, a Chicagoan of the Frank Lloyd Wright school, put the emphasis on coherent connections between the settings and the buildings, between landscape and cityscape. He died 20 years before his city could prove itself.

Canberra's name, which is said to be derived from "meeting place" in an Aboriginal tongue, was officially chosen in 1913 from among an outpouring of suggestions. Some serious people wanted a name as uplifting as Utopia or Shakespeare. Others devised classical inventions like Auralia and Austropolis. The most unusual proposal was a coinage designed to soothe every state capital: Sydmeladperbrisho. After that mouthful, the name Canberra came as a relief.

At the heart of the Australian Capital Territory, Canberra has a population of more than 250,000. Although an educational and research centre, it's essentially a company town; the local industry is government.

The ministries are here, and the parliament with its politicians, lobbyists and hangers-on, and the foreign embassies to add their exotic contribution. In spite of this considerable enterprise, Australia's only sizeable inland city is uncrowded and relaxed. So much green open space has been preserved, and so much inspired landscaping has gone on, that it looks as if they've hardly begun to exploit the place.

City Sights

There are several good ways to see Canberra, but not on foot. Pedestrians are out of luck in the great expanses of this city of parks. As on any map of Australia, the distances are longer than you think. So it's a good idea to sign up for a bus tour; they come in half-day and all-day versions. Or take the Explorer bus, which stops at all the main sights. You buy an all-day ticket, then hop on and off at will. Or you can drive yourself around town, following itineraries mapped out in a free sightseeing pamphlet. Motorists arriving from either Sydney or Melbourne can pick this up, along with leaflets, maps and advice, on the way into Canberra at the Visitor Information Centre, Northbourne Avenue, Dickson. In the middle of town the Canberra Visitor Centre can be found in the Jolimont Centre, Northbourne Avenue.

An effective starting place for a do-it-yourself tour of Canberra is **Regatta Point,** overlooking the lake that Burley Griffin cleverly created in the middle of town. The **Canberra Planning Exhibition** here uses three-dimensional mock-ups and audio-visual techniques to sum up the capital from its beginnings into the future. It's a painless orientation course.

Lake Burley Griffin, 35 kilometres (22 miles) around, is generously named after the town planner who realized the value of water for recreation as well as scenic beauty. You can tour the ins and outs of this man-made lake on sightseeing cruise boats. Or look into the fishing, sailing and windsurfing. Whooshing up from the lake, a giant **water jet** honours the explorer Captain Cook for several hours each day. The **Carillon,** another monument rising from Lake Burley Griffin (actually from a small island), was a gift from the British government. The music of its 53 bells, the biggest weighing six tons, can comfortably be heard

Australian National Gallery in Canberra: one of the capital's dynamic modern structures.

within a radius of 300 metres. Apart from concert recitals, it tells the time every 15 minutes, taking its tune from London's Big Ben.

North of the Lake

Canberra is older and greener than Brasília, and harder to navigate than an earlier "artificial" capital, Washington, D.C. To get the big picture, consider the view from the **Telecom Tower** atop Black Mountain. Millions of sightseers have paid to ascend the 195-metre (640-foot) tower for the 360° perspective. What with Canberra's pollution-free atmosphere, it's usually worth the investment, even at night, when the capital's public buildings are illuminated. Enclosed and open-air viewing platforms circle the structure towards the top. The designers couldn't resist adding a revolving restaurant.

On the eastern slopes of Black Mountain, the **National Botanic Gardens** are entirely devoted to Australian flora—the most comprehensive collection anywhere. In spite of Canberra's mostly mild, dry climate, rainforest specimens flourish under intensive care. Walter Burley Griffin was so fascinated by the native trees and plants that he put this place in his original plan.

The only part of the capital designed with pedestrians in mind is the area around the **Civic Centre.** The original business and shopping district opened in 1927—by Canberra standards that's ancient history—with symmetrical white colonnaded buildings in a mock-Spanish style. Nearby are modern shopping malls, the Canberra Theatre Centre, and a historic merry-go-round.

One of Canberra's best known landmarks, the **Australian Academy of Science**, is for looking and photographing but not for visiting. Architecturally, it's an interesting study in curves. The low-slung copper-plated dome rests on graceful arches standing in a circular moat. Some say it looks like a flying saucer at rest.

A more conventional dome covers the vast **Australian War Memorial,** a sandstone shrine climaxing a ceremonial avenue called **Anzac Parade.** There are war memorials all over Australia, but this is the definitive one. It's hard to avoid being swept up in the mood of the place as you walk past walls inscribed with the names of more than 100,000 Australian war dead. But beyond the heroic statues and mosaic murals, the memorial is a museum, with displays of uniforms through the years, battle maps, and plenty of hardware, from rifles to a real World War II Lancaster bomber.

Closer to the lake, one final military monument: the **Australian-American Memorial**, a slim aluminium shaft supporting a stylized eagle with its wings upheld in a V-for-victory mode. It was paid for by public contributions to acknowledge U.S. participation in the defence of Australia in World War II.

South of the Lake

The mostly windowless walls of the **Australian National Gallery** were designed to enclose "a museum of international significance", as official policy decreed. The enterprise has succeeded on several levels, showing off artists as varied as Monet and Matisse, Pollack and de Kooning, and an honour roll of Australian masters. Another indication of the range of interests: displays of art from Pacific island peoples, black Africa, and pre-Columbian America. A high point is the collection of Australian Aboriginal art: dreamily intricate human and animal forms on bark, evolving into the modern version in polymer paint on chipboard, dots and whorls and cross-hatching looking at first glance like arbitrary abstractions. The gallery's glistening garden of sculpture can't be seen from inside the building, according to plan, lest the patrons within be distracted.

The **High Court**, linked to the National Gallery by a footbridge, is a bold, boxy building with an immense expanse of glass on its façade. This last stop for legal appeals bears no resem-

---

Among Aussie Artists

Half a dozen among the names to remember in Australian art:

John Glover (1767–1849) arrived from England late in life. He caught the colours and sky of the young Australia.

Tom Roberts (1856–1931) brought to life the landscape and everyday activities of ordinary people in much-loved paintings.

Sir William Dobell (1899–1970) specialized in widely admired portraits; hostile critics considered them caricatures.

Albert Namatjira (1902–1959), an Aborigine, pictured his land in an artistic language the white man understood and admired.

Sir Russell Drysdale (1912–1981), English-born, saw the immense Outback and its characters through original eyes.

Sir Sydney Nolan (1917–) won the hearts of Australians with his series of perceptive paintings, notably the Ned Kelly series.

blance to the Victorian halls of justice elsewhere in the country. But it is no less impressive for its unconventional looks. The building's gigantic public hall is sometimes used for exhibitions and concerts.

Also on the lakefront, the **National Library** houses more than 2 million books—but not for browsing. This institution serves scholars and other libraries, not the drop-in reader. But you needn't feel totally excluded, for there are guided tours and exhibitions.

Embassy Row, the diplomatic quarter branching out well beyond the leafy suburb of Yarralumla, is a showcase of archi-

Brief encounter for an unlikely pair, in a Canberra pedestrian mall.

tectural vanities and charms, well worth a tour by car or sightseeing bus. In the early days of Canberra, diplomats dreaded the prospect of being transferred to the wilds, and most countries dragged their feet about moving until Prime Minister Menzies got tough in the 1950s. The United States was the first nation to open a legation in the new capital. Today's U.S. Embassy, on a hill, is a fine replica of an 18th-century American mansion. Many other nations also decided to erect buildings typical of their cultures, such as the Thai embassy with its sweeping roofs and the Indonesian compound adorned with statues of legendary figures. The Japanese embassy has a tea house in its formal garden.

Canberra's long-standingly temporary **Parliament House** became the seat of government in 1927. Considering its provisional nature, it had a high degree of understated dignity. The low-profile white stucco building is divided into three large halls, the Senate, the House of Representatives and Kings Hall. A new, permanent edifice was designed to replace old Parliament House in the bicentennial year of 1988. The winning project, which avoids monumental excess, blends into the side of Capital Hill, the site originally selected by Burley Griffin. The combination of unusual design and exploding building costs made the new complex a sure-fire cause célèbre.

Meanwhile, they're minting it in the south-western district called Deakin, and you can watch. The **Royal Australian Mint** has a visitors' gallery overlooking the production line where the country's coins are punched out. The factory also "moonlights" to produce the coins of several other countries. The Mint's own museum contains coins and medals of special value. If you're more attracted to hundred-dollar notes, you've come to the wrong fortress: Australia's paper money is printed in Melbourne.

Out of Town

Animal-lovers don't have far to go to meet kangaroos, echidnas, wombats and whatnot. The **Canberra Wildlife Gardens** are only a few miles south-east of the city centre, in Red Hill. The bird population includes parrots, kookaburras (the largest kingfishers), cockatoos and earthbound emus. A complement of animals to fondle rounds out the children's department.

The **Tidbinbilla Nature Reserve**, 40 kilometres (25 miles) south-west of Canberra, is a much bigger affair—thousands of acres of bushland where the native flora and fauna flourish.

Kangaroo fans can feed them in a reserve within the reserve.

Next to this unspoiled wilderness, the **Tidbinbilla Deep Space Tracking Station** takes advantage of its isolation, training its giant antenna on the most intriguing novelties of the cosmos. The Australian Department of Science operates the station on behalf of the U.S. space agency, NASA. Exhibitions on space exploration are open to the public.

A.C.T.'s Outpost

Thanks to a curious bit of gerrymandering, landlocked Canberra has a toehold on the South Pacific.

Jervis Bay, a peninsula on the New South Wales coast, was annexed to the Australian Capital Territory early in the 20th century on the off chance that the future Canberra might need a seaport. It didn't. The enclave today includes an uncommon combination of facilities: inviting dunes and beaches, the Royal Australian Naval College, a missile range, and a nature reserve.

One of the unusual sights is the wreck of the Cape St. George lighthouse. This 19th-century beacon suffered from one little defect: it was built in the wrong place, invisible to northbound ships. Worse, the construction itself was considered a hazard to navigation. The navy took aim and reduced it to a historic ruin.

QUEENSLAND

"Amazing Queensland", the admen trumpeted—and why not? It has just about everything that makes Australia so desirable, plus spectacular exclusives. Twice the size of Texas, sunsoaked Queensland gives you the choice of flashy tourist resorts, Outback mining towns or a modern metropolis, rainforest, desert or apple orchard. But the most amazing attraction of all is Queensland's offshore wonderland—the longest coral reef in the world, the Great Barrier Reef.

Queensland is one of those typical Australian success stories. It was founded in 1824 as a colony for incorrigible convicts, the "worst kind of felons", for whom not even the rigours of New South Wales were a deterrent. To quarantine criminality, free settlers were banned from a 50-mile radius. But adventurers, missionaries and hopeful immigrants couldn't be held back for long. Queensland's pastureland attracted eager squatters, and in 1867 the state joined the great Australian gold rush with a find of its own. Prosperity for all seemed just around the corner.

Mining still contributes generously to Queensland's economy. Above ground, the land is kind to cattle and sheep, and warmhearted crops like sugar, cotton, pineapples and bananas. Lately, tourism is reckoned to be the second biggest money-spinner. While the economy surges onward and upward, Queensland is controversial in political and social terms. The state government, proud of its reputation for arch-conservatism, has long been reviled by liberals, environmentalists, and Aboriginal rights activitists.

For touristic purposes the state can be divided into a dozen or more zones, from wild tropical adventurelands in the far north to the sophistication of the Gold Coast. The busiest gateway to all of this is Brisbane, the sprawling state capital.

BRISBANE

As befits a city with palm trees and backyard swimming pools, Brisbane's pace is so relaxed you'd hardly imagine its population was more than a million. The skyscrapers, some quite audacious, have gone a long way towards overcoming the "country-town" image, but enough of the old, elegant, low-slung buildings remain as a reminder; some are filigreed Victorian monuments, now done up in bright, defiant colours.

The climate is so welcoming that Brisbane has attracted immigrants from near and far. Just how far is indicated by the schedule of a local radio station, which broadcasts in, among other languages, Arabic, Bulgarian, Croatian, Fijian, Polish, Tongan and "Scandinavian".

In 1859, when Brisbane's population was all of 7,000, it became the capital of the newly proclaimed state of Queensland. The state treasury contained only 7½ pence; but within a couple of days even that was stolen. Old habits of the former penal colony seemed to die hard.

The capital's location, at a bend in the Brisbane River, has made possible some memorable floods over the years, but it sets an attractive stage for Australia's third largest city. Spanned by a network of bridges (the first dated 1930), the river continues through the suburbs to the beaches and islands of Moreton Bay. Some of Australia's most celebrated seafood comes from the bay, notably the gargantuan local mud crabs and the Moreton Bay bug. In spite of its name, this bug, related to the lobster, is a gourmet's joy.

71

City Sights

To begin with the historic heart of town, Brisbane's neoclassical **City Hall** is easy to find because of its inspired spire, 91 metres (nearly 300 feet) tall. One of the foundation stones was laid by the Prince of Wales in 1920. You can mount the great clock tower for what is still a hard-to-beat panorama. The building also houses a museum and art gallery.

Up the hill, on Wickham Terrace, stands an unusual historic building, the **Old Windmill**, also known as the Old Observatory, built by convicts in 1829. Design problems foiled the windmill idea; to grind the colony's grain, the energy of the wind had to be replaced by a convict-powered treadmill. Later, the tower found less strenuous uses as a fire lookout station and a transmitter for early television experiments.

King George Square, next to City Hall, and the nearby **Anzac Square** are typical of the green open spaces that make the centre of town breathable. The pedestrian traffic is so heavy here that it's regulated by a line built down the middle of the paving; keep left.

Pedestrians-only is the rule in Brisbane's central **Queen Street Mall**, flanked by big stores and interspersed with shady refuges and outdoor cafés. This is a crucial place for people-watching. On a fine day, visitors from cooler climes should take a seat and watch the lively parade of girls, tan and fit, in brightly coloured dresses. The local men go about unselfconsciously in sport shirts and shorts—except for the businessmen, wilting in suits and ties. The little restaurants and takeaway cafés feature everything from ethnic curiosities to "gourmet hotdogs".

Where central Brisbane fits into the bend in the river, the **Botanic Gardens** green the peninsula with countless species of Australian and "exotic" (such as American) trees, plants and flowers. A political hothouse, the 19th-century Renaissance-style **Parliament House** overlooking the gardens, is the headquarters of the state's legislative assembly.

Across the Victoria Bridge from the centre of town, the **Queensland Cultural Centre** puts most of Brisbane's cultural eggs in one lavish, modern basket. The south bank complex includes the Queensland Art Gallery, a 2,000-seat concert hall and a comparable theatre, plus the state museum. Riverside gardens, plazas, restaurants and cafés round off the glittering scene. There are guided tours of the art gallery as well as the Performing Arts Complex.

To escape the heat and rush of the city, try **Mount Coot-tha Forest Park,** on the south-west

edge of Brisbane. The name is derived from an Aboriginal word meaning "mountain of dark native honey". The spacious park features a giant modern dome enclosing some 200 species of tropical plants. Here, too, you'll find Australia's largest **Planetarium.**

By car, bus or taxi, it's only about 11 kilometres (7 miles) to **Lone Pine Sanctuary,** with one of the country's best known collections of native animals. By boat the trip is a few miles longer. The stars of the show are the koalas, mostly sleeping like babies, clinging to their eucalyptus branches. They are awakened now and then to pose for photos in the arms of tour-

Pages 72–73: Brisbane filigree.
Above: Central city skyscrapers.

ists. They "perform" by riding on the back of a German shepherd dog. The sanctuary has kangaroos galore; they are so tame they come up to you to be fed and, if you insist, petted. You can also get a close-up look at a couple of Tasmanian devils, which are red-eared, piggish-looking marsupials and, unlike the koalas, frankly difficult to love.

GOLD COAST

South of Brisbane, at day-trip distance if you're rushed, the Gold Coast is a Down Under impression of Miami Beach. It may be overexploited, but it's so dynamic and there's so much to do that you can hardly fault it. And the beach—anything from 30 to 50 kilometres of it, depending who's measuring—is a winner in any league.

Funny-faced Koalas

The cuddliest creature in Australia is the koala, Queensland's official state mascot, a marsupial sometimes mistaken for a small bear.

Until the government put the koala on the list of protected national treasures, heartless hunters used to slaughter them for their fur.

With its big fluffy ears, beady eyes and black rubbery nose, the koala looks too funny to take seriously. It has only one obvious interest in life: the consumption of eucalyptus leaves. The pungent odour of the gum oil permeates the animal's body, giving it antiseptic protection and repelling predators. Some say the overdose of gum oil intoxicates the little addicts, which is why they sleep most of the day.

Like the kangaroo, the koala produces an unfinished baby that matures in the mother's pouch (which has the opening towards the rear). Baby koalas remain tied to the maternal apron strings for almost four years. Koala fathers, engrossed in the nonstop eucalyptus feast, ignore their familial responsibilities.

The trip down the Pacific Highway from Brisbane is a study in Australian escapism. In the midst of forest and brushland grows a seemingly inexhaustible supply of amusement or theme parks. They lure transient fun-seekers with attractions for all the family: "computerised animated koala show", "log ride splashdown", and "sheep shearing exhibitions". These diverting parks have names like Dreamworld, Magic Mountain, Lion Safari, Sheep Station and Old MacDonald's Farm. The Gold Coast War Museum advertises "free uniform hire". You enter the "Great White Shark Expo" through monstrous open jaws.

Lunch at the lakeside after a fishing expedition.

The essence of the Gold Coast is **Surfers Paradise,** as lively as any seaside resort in the world. When you're not sunbathing, swimming or, of course, surfing, you can wander through the malls, window-shopping, eating out and socializing. Or go waterskiing or parasailing. Or take a joy ride in an ancient Tiger Moth. Or a "moonlight booze cruise". The pace is hectic, and the revelry goes on as late as you can last.

Surfers Paradise is approached through a thicket of petrol stations, fast-food outlets and motels—a reconstruction of the outskirts of many an American city, and in similar taste. The conglomeration is skyscrapered in an odd way: tall, slim apartment blocks interspersed with bungalows. It's not a real

city at all, except for the pursuit of fun. (Until 1933 the community was known less glamorously as Elston.) The tanned, relaxed "beautiful people" you see on the beach today were pale yokels a couple of days ago; the irresistible sun does wonders.

By way of nature-oriented Gold Coast attractions, **Seaworld** stars frolicking dolphins, with the villainous parts played by performing sharks. At the **Currumbin Bird Sanctuary,** huge flocks of brilliantly coloured lorikeets, shrilly chorusing, come to greet the tourists—when food is being served.

Currumbin is down towards the southern edge of the Gold

A high-rise mirage on the horizon: Surfers Paradise.

Coast, which ends at Point Danger (so named by Captain Cook when he passed by in 1770). Beyond lies New South Wales. The modest danger on the N.S.W. side of the line—and the reason the area is so popular with tourists from Brisbane—is the availability of mass gambling opportunities. South of the border the one-armed bandits, or poker machines ("pokies" for short), are kept so busy the cheery clang of coins never stops.

SUNSHINE COAST

For the beachy perfection of the Gold Coast minus most of the commercialism, try the resorts of the Sunshine Coast, north of Brisbane. Some of Australia's best surfing is hiding here.

Inland, the territory is laden with vast plantations of sugar cane, bananas, pineapples and passionfruit. The area is also a centre of production of the prized macadamia nut, named after a 19th-century Australian scientist, John Macadam.

The Sunshine Coast resort closest to Brisbane, **Caloundra**, has a beach for every tide. For the historically minded, a less-than-fullscale replica of Captain Cook's ship *Endeavour* may be visited. And a local museum of "matchcraft" specializes in models painstakingly constructed from thousands of matchsticks.

The northernmost town on the Sunshine Coast, **Noosa**, used to be a hideaway of fishermen, surfers and beachcombers, but it has been discovered by the trendsetters from Sydney and Melbourne. Noosa National Park, a sanctuary of rainforest and underpopulated beaches, occupies the dramatic headland that protects Laguna Bay from the sometimes squally South Pacific breezes. Fraser Island (see p. 82) is easily reached from here.

Near **Nambour**, the principal town inland from the Sunshine Coast, you can hardly miss a terribly Australian sort of tourist attraction: the monstrously magnified symbol. A startling example is an immense reproduction of a pineapple, as tall as a house—the come-on for a whole tourist complex. A competitor in this field of culture is The Big Cow, so colossal that you are invited to climb inside. Collectors of kitsch can find additional excesses in the area.

GREAT BARRIER REEF

Viewed from above, Australia's biggest, most wonderful sight looks like a re-enactment of the beginning of the world. Just below the ocean waves, millions of minuscule cells multiply relentlessly in fantastic shapes. Growing into an infinite variety of forms—and colours from lettuce green to flaming red—they comprise the world's largest living phenomenon. The Great Barrier Reef stretches as far as you can see and beyond: more than 2,000 kilometres (1,200 miles) of submerged tropical gardens. In among them, the sea is sprinkled with hundreds of paradise islands.

Seen more intimately through a skin-diver's mask, the Great Barrier Reef is the spectacle of a lifetime, like being inside a boundless tropical fishbowl among the most lurid specimens ever conceived. The fanciful shapes of the coral, gently waving in the tide, might almost lull

you to sleep. But not for long. A blazing blue and red fish darts into sight, pursuing a cloud of a thousand minnows. A sea urchin stalks past on its needles; a giant clam opens its hairy mouth as if sighing with nostalgia for its youth, a century ago.

In 1770 Captain Cook, who was exploring the Australian coast, stumbled upon the Great Barrier Reef. The *Endeavour* was gored by an unsuspected outcrop of coral. Patching the holes as best they could, the crew managed to sail across the barrier, and the vessel limped onto the beach at what is now Cooktown, where major repairs had to be improvised.

There are many ways of appreciating the coral and its fishy visitors. You can stay dry in a glass-bottomed boat, or join a brief cruise aboard a semi-submarine. Or descend into an underwater observatory. If you prefer to remain topside, at certain places and tides you can walk—but not barefoot!—on the coral as it stands exposed. With a mask and snorkel tube you can get close to the whole truth of the underwater world. But the only way to blend totally with the environment is in a weightless state, diving as long and as deep as you please with scuba gear. If you're not a qualified diver you can take a crash course at one of the resorts.

The Living Reef

When the conditions are just right—when the sea is clear, warm and not too deep—the coral reef builds itself.

The reef is a living organism, the work of millions of minute polyps building on the skeletons of their ancestors. They grow into surreal formations, such as elkhorn, swaying seafans or a wrinkled brain. The coral feeds on, and in turn feeds, microscopic algae. The oxygen-producing algae support schools of theatrically tinted fish, like angelfish, butterfly fish and red emperors. These beauties attract the whoppers that fishermen dream of. It all seems a beautiful, intricate master plan.

The Resort Islands

The reef—actually a formation of thousands of neighbouring clumps of reefs—runs close to shore in the north of Queensland but slants ever farther out to sea as it extends southwards. Hundreds of islands are scattered across the protected waters between the coral barrier and the mainland. More than a dozen have been developed into resorts, ranging from spartan to sybaritic. But only three resort islands—Heron, Green and Lizard—are on the reef itself. From all the others you have to travel, by sea or air, from 5 to 70 kilometres (3 to 40 miles) to reach the main attraction.

Here are some details about the character and facilities of the resorts of the Great Barrier Reef, reading from south to north.

Fraser Island is actually south of the Great Barrier Reef but close enough to it, and interesting enough, to rate inclusion in this list. About 120 kilometres (75 miles) long, Fraser is considered the largest sand island in the world. But there's more than sand: lakes, marsh, pine forest and rainforest. This is an island for fishing and beachcombing, not swimming or coral dives. Excursions to the island are available from Noosa (see p. 80).

Lady Elliot Island is a coral isle, part of the reef, but south of the Tropic of Capricorn. Activities centre on diving, reef walks, swimming and windsurfing. The gateway airport is Bundaberg, a sugar-producing town 375 kilometres (230 miles) up the coast from Brisbane.

Heron Island is heaven for divers. It's a small coral island right on the Great Barrier Reef. Amazing coral and hundreds of species of fish are waiting to be sighted just outside your door. Alternatively, nature lovers can concentrate on the giant green turtles, which waddle ashore between mid-October and March to bury their eggs in the sand. Heron Island is also the goal of thousands of migrating noddy terns and shearwaters. You can fly to Heron by helicopter in half an hour from Gladstone.

Great Keppel Island is one of the larger resort islands in area and in holiday population. The great white beaches are simply gorgeous. The Great Barrier Reef is fully 70 kilometres (more than 40 miles) away, but Great Keppel is surrounded by good local coral, and there's an underwater observatory. For other angles on the sea's secrets in the area, try a glass-bottomed boat, snorkelling or scuba-diving.

Between Queensland coast and the Reef, emerald islands litter the sea.

Feathers and fins in the island resorts. Overleaf: Dunk denizens.

Brampton Island, an informal resort, is easily reached by air or sea from Mackay. With forested mountains and abundant wildlife, it's worth exploring the interior of the island. You can also discover neighbouring Carlisle Island, connected to Brampton by a reef which is wadeable when the tide's out. If the many sandy beaches don't suffice, there's a salt-water swimming pool.

Lindeman Island has an airstrip and a golf course on its plateau, from which the view over the Whitsunday Passage is highly recommended. Most activities are available, and like Dunk and Magnetic islands, it can offer horse-riding. Lindeman Island has recently been refurbished and upgraded as a holiday destination, with the emphasis on comfort rather than size.

Hamilton Island. With its jet airstrip, 14-storey apartment tower, seven restaurants, ten bars and what's called the largest freshwater pool in the Pacific, Hamilton is the slickest international resort in the Coral Sea. It's all carefully thought out, from the busy yacht marina and shops to the landscaping around the Polynesian-style cottages.

Divers can rush out to the reef aboard the "world's fastest passenger-carrying catamaran" or by helicopter. The island's rainbow lorikeets not only eat out of your hand but sit on your arm while doing it. There are tame kangaroos, too.

Long Island, close to the mainland and far from the reef, is long and narrow and hilly. It's best known as the site of the Whitsunday 100 resort, designed to attract 18- to 35-year-old holiday-makers with fun and games, music and romance. Elsewhere on the lush island are ideal sandy beaches and modest facilities for non-swingers.

South Molle Island, one of the bigger resorts, has every imaginable recreational facility except, at last report, horse-riding. Fitness enthusiasts have the use of a gym, a sauna, a spa, and a swimming pool suitable for serious workouts as well as cooling dips. The beaches are good, and there are interesting paths for walks through the hilly bush. The Great Barrier Reef, though, is some 60 kilometres (nearly 40 miles) away.

Daydream Island. The tiniest of all the Barrier Reef resort islands, Daydream snoozes just off shore from busy Shute Harbour. Since beaches are not the island's strongest selling point, they've built a swimming pool.

There is accommodation for a few hundred guests.

Hayman Island is the most northerly of the Whitsunday group. (Predictably, it was Captain Cook who named the archipelago after the feast of Pentecost, which is approximately when he passed through.) Recently redeveloped as a chic, international-class resort, Hayman has a marina for drop-in yachts, and a choice of restaurants, bars and shops. The long, sandy beach suggests all sorts of water sports, dutifully catered for by the resort's activities staff. Some tiny, uninhabited isles are so close you can walk out to them at low tide.

Magnetic Island is virtually a suburb of Townsville, the biggest city in northern Queensland. Many of its 2,000 permanent residents commute to work on the mainland by ferry. Being so easy to reach, it's a busy day-trip destination—by sea or helicopter. But Magnetic Island also has plenty of accommodation of all classes. Most of the island is a national park, busy with birds and animals. The choice of beaches is enticing. Magnetic Island, "Maggie" to the locals, got its name from the omnipresent Captain Cook, whose compass broke down here.

Orpheus Island. The way to get to this exclusive resort is by seaplane from Townsville; on the way you'll get an aerial introduction to the expanse and brilliance of the reef. Orpheus has all the facilities the most demanding guests might desire, including golf, tennis, waterskiing, sailing and windsurfing. Children under 12 are barred.

Hinchinbrook Island basks in a superlative of its own: "The world's largest island national park." A continental rather than coral island, but only 5 kilometres (3 miles) from the reef, Hinchinbrook has a couple of camp sites (park rangers issue permits on the mainland) and a small, plain resort. Inland from the smooth sand beaches are mountains worth climbing, rainforest, waterfalls, and bush in which you'll come across wallabies.

Bedarra Island, in the Family Islands group, has a very small, exclusive resort on its west coast. It's reachable via neighbouring Dunk Island. The nearest mainland town is Tully, noted for its annual rainfall average, the highest in the country. Statistically, Tully is twice as wet as Darwin.

Dunk Island is mostly a national park. But one of the best developed resorts fits inoffensively into a corner of the island originally occupied by a World War II radar station. Guests enjoy a big range of diversions from cricket, golf and tennis to waterskiing and tobogganing.

Dunk's genuine tropical rainforest offers a taste of the eternal: vines struggling to grab the sunlight at the expense of the trees they strangle on the way up. All is silence except for a waterfall, the trickle of raindrops off glistening leaves, the fluttering wings of a brightly plumed bird.

Fitzroy Island came into the resort business later than most. Like Green Island, it's the object of day excursions from Cairns. Accommodation is quite limited, but a dining room and evening entertainment keep the overnight population amused. Fitzroy Island's interior is rainforest; the beaches meet anyone's standards.

Green Island, one of the three resorts actually on the reef, is popular with day-trippers from Cairns, but when the crowds depart, the vacationers occupying its small colony of cabins and lodge units have the tiny island, and its throngs of sea-birds, to themselves. Green Island's Underwater Observatory, claiming to be the first of its kind in the world, lets you view the coral garden from a dry vantage point three fathoms deep. In this situation, the fish come to look through the glass at humans in the tank. Another attraction, a short walk inland, is a Marineland with crocodiles and giant turtles.

Lizard Island. Lying about 30 kilometres (less than 20 miles) off the tropical northern coast of Queensland, Lizard has all the trappings of a fictional escape island: rainforest, mangrove swamps and a couple of dozen delectable beaches. The island is almost on the edge of one of Australia's most productive game-fishing zones, where the half-ton black marlin live. Favoured by millionaires and celebrities, Lizard has almost every vacation facility—golf, tennis, windsurfing, sailing—except a nightclub. Which is just the way the guests like it.

Perils of the Shallows

Now for the bad news—reef walkers have to beware of perils in paradise. Some types of coral can give you a very unpleasant burn. And hidden where you least expect to step on one is the stonefish, a camouflaged beast with poisonous spines that lives on the sea bottom. Stout boots are the only defence.

Between December and March or April an even more serious threat stalks the mainland coast of northern Queensland: an invasion of sea wasps, or box jellyfish. Virtually invisible as it floats aimlessly near the beach, the sea wasp has poisonous stingers that can kill in 30 seconds. If the locals are boycotting what looks like irresistible surf, a plague of the venomous drifters may explain why. Resist!

TROPICAL COAST

The coast of mainland Queensland paralleling the Barrier Reef is a fiercely difficult drive along a highway that looks easy on the map. Here are a few highlights, from south to north, heading relentlessly towards the Equator.

Rockhampton sits only a few kilometres north of the Tropic of Capricorn—23°27' south of the Equator, the line that officially divides the tropics from the subtropics. From here on northwards, you need no excuse to order an icy beer to assuage your tropical thirst. Rockhampton, known as the beef capital of Australia, has some genuinely interesting Victorian architecture, worth a walking tour.

Mackay is the next substantial town, and even by Australian standards it's a long haul—about 340 kilometres (more than 210 miles)—over Highway 1, a road not particularly noted for its comfort or scenery. Surrounded by dense green fields of cane, Mackay processes one-third of the nation's sugar crop. At the harbour you can tour the world's biggest bulk sugar terminal. Inland from Mackay, in rugged mountain country, is the largest national park in Queensland, **Eungella National Park.** This is probably the only place in Australia where you can see platypuses in the wild. The best time is morning and late afternoon.

Proserpine, another sugar town, is inland from **Airlie Beach** and **Shute Harbour,** lively resorts from which there are boat trips to the Whitsunday Islands.

Another 265 kilometres (165 miles) closer to the Equator, and you're in Australia's largest tropical city, **Townsville,** named after one Robert Towns, a Sydneysider. With a population close to 100,000, Townsville is the headquarters of the mining and cattle industries of Queensland's interior and a gateway for islands of the Reef. The historic centre of town, along the river, contains some photogenic old buildings with filigreed iron balconies or stately columns and arches. Townsville is proud of its broad modern pedestrian mall, enlivened by exotic birds inhabiting the tropical trees. And for the ultimate touch of sophistication, a big, glamorous gambling casino stands on reclaimed land along the bay.

Less than half as big as Townsville, the metropolis of Queensland's far north, **Cairns,** is a cheerful, thriving port laid out in grid style with huge blocks and extra-wide streets. Thanks largely to its tourist throngs, the town is full of life, day and night. The excitement begins

*Kuranda railway station—
a green extravaganza.*

early in the morning, when the speedy catamarans leave for Green Island and the smaller boats set sail with scuba divers or fishermen aboard. Big-game fishing is big business in Cairns, where the sportsmen hunt black marlin.

Along the Coral Seafront, a spacious Esplanade, shaded by lavish banyans and palms, aims to compensate for the muddy state of the shallow sea here. In a go-ahead town like Cairns the travel agencies open their doors at 7.30 a.m. and keep going until after dark. They sell a fat collection of excursions—to Green Island, inland to Kuranda and the Atherton Tableland, and up the coast as far as Port Douglas.

Kuranda, a charming little tourist town, is best reached by colourful narrow-gauge train. Leaving Cairns and the steamy sugar-cane fields, the century-old right-of-way climbs to cooler temperatures, alternating between tunnels and scenic mountainsides, loveliest at Barron Falls gorge. At the end of the line, the Kuranda rail station is a classic in itself, bedecked with potted ferns and tropical plants. The village is well supplied with souvenir shops, cafés, restaurants and other attractions, including a mini-museum of Aboriginal history and art.

Spectacularly beautiful coastal scenery is the reward along the highway north from Cairns to **Port Douglas.** The perfect beaches along the way are so underpopulated you can easily have one to yourself. When the tide goes out, Port Douglas's **Four Mile Beach** is a wide, hard-packed, almost flat sweep of sand suitable for bike races, jogging, or simply sunbathing.

For practical purposes, the nearby sugar-milling town of

Mossman is the end of the line. From here northwards it's several hundred hot kilometres of mostly rough driving to the likeable river port of **Cooktown,** where Captain Cook's battered *Endeavour* was beached in 1770. The James Cook Memorial Museum tells all about it.

The tip of Cape York Peninsula, north of Cooktown, is a vast expanse of marshy terrain, prone to flooding and crocodiles, and negotiable only by the most intrepid adventurers in well-equipped four-wheel drive vehicles. The rivers are totally impassable from December to March; Coen is the last outpost for supplies and fuel.

There's always room for more on the Port Douglas shore.

NORTHERN TERRITORY

On the surface, the Northern Territory might seem an unpromising tourist destination. Its deserts, torrid tablelands and rainforests look immensely uninviting. Especially when it's blazing hot. But the wildlife is enchanting, the scenery magnificent, and the people, though few and far between, welcome the wandering stranger with Outback hospitality and charm.

The population of the self-governing territory is only around 125,000. About a quarter of all Territorians are Aborigines, so cultural insights are part of the agenda for foreign visitors. This is the place to find the grandeur and mystery of the most sacred Aboriginal sites.

The Northern Territory covers about one-sixth of Australia's total area. The climate effectively divides the N.T. into two parts: the north, called "The Top End", is jungly and very hot. The rest of the Territory, known as "The Centre", has drastically less rainfall. The red Centre, with its infinite horizons and parched, rugged beauty, fits the stereotype of "Back of Beyond".

DARWIN

Australia's northernmost port, the capital and only real city of the Northern Territory, revels in the tropical sun and every sport under it, from cricket and baseball to sailing and parasailing. The young, prosperous city radiates the optimism of the reborn, for Darwin has survived far more than its share of catastrophes. At a cost of hundreds of lives, it was bombed scores of times in World War II. Rebuilt, it was wiped out by a killer cyclone in 1974. The planners went back to the drawing board to design a bigger and better city.

Darwin's daytime temperature averages more than 30 °C (86 °F) virtually all year round. But while transients wilt, the locals know how to withstand the heat. They dress lightly and casually —even businessmen wear shorts to work—and down a record amount of frosty beer to stave off dehydration. Elsewhere in

Spindly trees hang on for dear life in Standley Chasm.

Australia a "stubby" means a small beer; order a "stubby" in Darwin and you get a two litre bottle—almost half a gallon. This gives a clue to the Darwin sense of humour; and the jokes are a pleasant distraction from the heavy-handed heat. Empty beer cans wind up as the construction material for a flotilla of fanciful boats competing in Darwin's annual slapstick regatta.

Local chauvinists admit that Darwin, which is about 3,000 kilometres (nearly 2,000 miles) from Sydney and Perth, is "a trifle isolated". But that doesn't seem to deter the eager newcomers arriving from all parts of the country. Darwin's population grows three times faster than the national average.

City Sights

Historic buildings are the last thing you'd expect to find in a city wiped out by a modern cyclone. But visitors are taken on a tour of restored 19th-century buildings calling to mind the atmosphere of the pioneering days. Darwin's foundation as a permanent settlement dates back only to 1869, relatively modern history even by Australian standards.

Government House, overlooking the harbour, is an elegant example of colonial style. A series of cyclones and the wartime bombs badly damaged the building (known as the Seven Gables), but it has been put back together in fine form, and is surrounded by lovely tropical gardens.

Dating from 1885, the single-storey building called **Brown's Mart** is now a theatre for live plays. You might say the building has a theatrically chequered past. Built as a miner's exchange, it was converted for use as a police station and subsequently served the community as a brothel.

Also on an offbeat historical theme, the old **Fannie Bay Gaol** opened for business in 1883. Closed down in 1952, the jail is now a museum, where you can follow the march of penal progress since those rough-and-ready days. The gallows were last used in 1952.

Other restored buildings include the **Victoria Hotel,** as Victorian as its name, and the former **Admiralty House,** now an art gallery. A surviving portion of the old Anglican **Christ Church Cathedral** has been incorporated into the soaring modern building.

The New Darwin

For the feel of modern Darwin, drift over to the **Smith Street Mall,** a pedestrians-only shopping area in the heart of the restored city. Here you'll find the government tourist bureau,

with maps, brochures and advice. The shady mall, lined with stores, cafés and restaurants, is the perfect place for people-watching. This may be your first close-up look at Aboriginal people, who often congregate in the mall. If you want to take a photo, be discreet; they don't normally appreciate this kind of attention. Neither, for that matter, do the white Australian "characters"

Theatre, shopping centre and hotel, all in one, in go-ahead Darwin.

who turn up here with "Outback" all but written on their beards.

Darwin's **Performing Arts Centre,** an enterprising post-Modernist edifice designed for the tropics, puts theatre, shops, cafés and a hotel under one roof. Another building that looks re-

97

markably ambitious for a town of Darwin's size is the **Diamond Beach Casino,** a white pyramid of a leisure centre surrounding the magnet of gambling. Investors have a choice of traditional games in the sophisticated mould of Monte-Carlo or the more folksy Australian style. You can try your hand at two-up, the Australian game that's as simple as tossing two coins. The excitement grabs participants and hangers-on alike.

Lovers of tropical flowers will be delighted by every little garden around town, but the ultimate display occupies the **Botanical Gardens,** 34 hectares (84 acres) of the most fetching,

Nonchalant noonday cowboy on a Territorian corral.

fragrant flowers and plants. In addition to the bougainvillea and frangipani, the orchids are a special source of pride.

Back to the seaside for something completely different: Doctors Gully, at the end of the Esplanade, is the site of a strange audience-participation ritual, the feeding of the fish. At an establishment called **Aquascene**, tourists wade into the sea at high tide (check the local paper for the time) to hand-feed catfish, mullet, bream and other sizeable denizens of the harbour. Thousands of fish turn up here daily for the festivities, returning to deep-sea pursuits until the next free hand-out.

If you'd prefer not to get your feet wet, Darwin has an unusual aquarium, **Indo-Pacific Marine.** It's said to be one of only four of its kind in the world, containing living coral reef communities transplanted from the sea.

Overlooking Fannie Bay, surrounded by gardens, the Northern Territory **Museum of Arts and Sciences** is the place for a quick briefing on Aboriginal art and culture. It's also strong on archaeology and the natural sciences.

Other cities are built around a central business district or a park, but Darwin stretches in all directions around its airport. This is handy for airline passengers but less so for the locals, who must go miles out of their way to get from one part of town to another on opposite sides of the runway.

On the north side of the airport, near the Casuarina High School, is a moving **monument** to the victims of Cyclone Tracy, which killed more than 50 people on Christmas Eve, 1974. It's a "sculpture" of twisted iron girders, like roller-coaster tracks gone wild. No artist produced this abstraction; it's merely the way three girders were contorted when the big wind destroyed a nearby house.

Cyclone Tracy taught everyone a lesson in architecture and

Not on Your Life

When Darwin's weather is at its most sweltering—from October to May—a dip in the sea ought to be just what the doctor ordered, right?

Wrong, fatally wrong.

Nature has played a very unkind trick on this part of the Timor Sea. Throngs of sinister sea wasps, otherwise known as box jellyfish, arrive in the southern summer. They can kill, or at least cause a most unpleasant shock. It's the season to stay ashore.

When the slippery sea monsters have drifted back to their more northerly haunts, there are a few other little problems for swimmers and divers. For instance, sharks.

engineering. Now specially rein-
forced roof construction is required by law; houses should
never again go sailing away.
Even Darwin's **Chinese Temple,**
notwithstanding its sweeping
roofs, is guaranteed cyclone-
proof. It serves Buddhists, Tao-
ists and Confucians.

East of Darwin

In the tropical wilderness east of
Darwin you can see natural phenomena called **"magnetic ant-
hills"**, scattered like prehistoric
dolmens in the bush alongside
the highway. "Magnetic ant-
hills" is a neat expression de-
scribing the insect equivalent of
skyscrapers. But, to be accurate,
they are neither magnetic nor
ant-hills. These termite mounds,
often taller than humans, are
always aligned exactly north-
south ... for reasons only termites can explain. They look like
two-dimensional sand-castles.

Fogg Dam, 60 kilometres
(37 miles) east of Darwin, is a
splendid sanctuary for a dozen
species of water bird, coexisting
on magical pools. This was the
site of the Humpty Doo rice
project, a multi-million-dollar
scheme to grow rice without the
disadvantages of the traditional feet-in-the-mud, aching-back
method. According to the plan
devised by the efficiency experts,
airplanes effortlessly seeded the
area at one fell swoop. Countless
swarms of birds, not having been
consulted, feasted on this manna
from heaven as soon as the seeds
hit the ground. Riceless, Humpty
Doo had a great fall and went
out of business. The area is again
strictly for the birds.

*Magnetic anthills dwarf tourists
in the bush east of Darwin.*

✶KAKADU NATIONAL PARK

Birdwatchers, botanists and all other visitors are enthralled by Kakadu National Park, about 220 kilometres (175 miles) east of Darwin. The scenery ranges from romantic to awesome. As an unparalleled outdoor museum of ancient Aboriginal art, the park is on the World Heritage List of places of "outstanding universal value" deserving protection. Timeless paintings on Kakadu's rock ledges brim with mystery and meaning. Some have been there since the era of Europe's Paleolithic cave art.

Nineteen different clans of Aborigines live in the park's 6,144 square kilometres (2,372 square miles), between the Wild Man and the East Alligator rivers. They lease the land to the

National Parks and Wildlife Service and participate in the park's management; you'll see Aborigines in the uniform of park rangers.

Nature has bluntly divided Kakadu into two worlds: the plains, with their lagoons and creeks, and the escarpment, a stark sandstone wall marking the western edge of Arnhem Land. From the high plateau, waterfalls tumble to the lowlands in the wet season (November to March). The floodplains entertain water birds by the thousand. The names alone turn laymen into dedicated birdwatchers: white-throated grasswren, white-lined honeyeater and white-breasted whistler, to list but three of the species that breed in the park. The star of the show, though, is the jabiru, a stately variety of stork.

In the mangroves you'll see striated heron, little kingfisher, and broad-billed flycatcher. And you can go down the checklist with magpie goose, black shag, ibis and crested plover. A special delight is the sight of the delicately poised lotus bird, which walks miraculously on the water.

The waterways are rich in the eminently edible barramundi. Less appetizingly, the estuaries are home to the saltwater crocodile, which preys on barramundi, birds, small animals and, on special occasions, humans.

Kakadu's Rock Art

At as many as a thousand different places in the park, ancient Aborigines left works of art—rock paintings in styles both primitive and eerily sophisticated.

The earliest legacy consists of arrangements of handprints and the imprints of objects that were dyed and thrown for decorative effect at cliff walls and cave ceilings. Many centuries later,

abstract-expressionist artists re-invented a similar splashy technique.

The next generation of prehistoric artists concentrated on the figures of animals. Among them is a curious variety of anteater believed to have become extinct perhaps 18,000 years ago, a valuable clue to the age of some of these paintings. The same school of artists painted stickfigure humans in hunting and

Pages 102–103 and above:
Paintings by nature and paintings
by men, in Kakadu.

battle scenes. They used ochre pigments for colour.

Later artists brought movement to their pictures—for instance, hunters caught in the act of throwing spears or boomerangs. An innovation of this era

105

was the use of abstract marks around certain figures, like a modern cartoonist's squiggles representing a character's surprise or fear.

A few thousand years after this, Aboriginal artists developed a remarkable style, now called X-ray painting. The profile of, say, a fish is clearly painted but instead of its scales we see its bones and internal organs, with the emphasis on edible or otherwise useful parts.

After Australia was colonized, the white man, too, became a subject for Aboriginal artists. There are pictures of the sailing ships the British arrived in, and caricatures, scarcely flattering, of the new settlers holding recognizable muskets.

KATHERINE GORGE

The most spectacular natural attraction of the Top End of the Northern Territory, Katherine Gorge is about 350 kilometres (220 miles) "down the Track" from Darwin. "The Track" is what they call the highway linking the Timor Sea and Alice Springs, in the Red Centre of Australia. Originally a rough path fit for bullock carts and camel trains servicing the overland telegraph line, the route was upgraded by the Americans in World War II to supply Darwin, which was dangerously isolated and under attack.

Katherine, to be precise, is not a single gorge but a series of 13 gorges. During the wet season (from November to March) the

---

Creepy Crocs

The saltwater crocodiles found in relative abundance in Kakadu National Park eat anything they can wrap their teeth around. Every so often they devour a boatsman, bather or wader, or someone who comes too close to the bank of a river or marsh. Although they grow to a length of 3 or 4 metres (10 to 13 feet), "salties" often escape notice as they snooze almost submerged in a swamp.

You may feel no great affection for the earth's largest living reptiles, but don't pester them. Crocodiles are protected by Australian law.

torrents, waterfalls, whirlpools and rapids give an impression of thundering power. But it's uncomfortably hot and humid, and sometimes the nonstop rains cut off the roads. So Katherine Gorge National Park is best visited in the dry season (April to October), when the water flows at a relative trickle. Flat-bottomed boats cruise the river, which reflects sheer cliffsides; walks and hikes offer other perspectives.

Among the sights are Aboriginal wall-paintings portraying kangaroos and other native animals bigger than life-size. Live kangaroos may be seen in the park, as well as the echidna (spiny anteater) and the dingo. Adding a tremor of excitement, there are glimpses of a freshwater variety of crocodile called Johnstone's Crocodile. Unlike the "salties" of the north, though, these fierce-looking reptiles are timid fish-eaters; tourists do not figure on their menu. Bird life is colourful: hooded parrots, black cockatoos, and agile rainbow birds.

ALICE SPRINGS

A set of traffic lights has slightly tamed the adventurous Outback atmosphere of Alice Springs, the biggest town for a thousand miles around. "The Alice" looks like the frontier town you imagined: a relaxed, friendly,

---

1880s Anthropology

In recent times, the "romance" of Aboriginal culture, the spiritual link with ancestors and the environment, has fascinated tourists as well as anthropologists. But in Queen Victoria's days, the view was darker.

A tome published in London in the early 1880s (The Races of Mankind) describes Australia's indigenous people as "acute thieves, treacherous in the extreme, greedy, capricious, cunning, unreasoning, passionate and cruel." Aiming for objectivity, the author, Scottish naturalist Dr. Robert Brown, adds that the Aborigine's character was not improved by contact with the white settlers and stockmen, "who are, as a rule, by no means the most polished of their species."

Dr. Brown reports that the native "is never without some private squabble or vendetta on his hand, but wars proper are unknown to him. They would require foresight and powers of organisation of which these savages are not possessed; his intellect is too low for this."

Aboriginal marriage customs—starting with caveman-style head-bashing and abduction by brute force of the prospective bride—were considered so unspeakable that a British ethnologist of the era felt constrained to write about the subject in Latin.

slightly dishevelled community of pioneers, dreamers, transients ... and throngs of tourists.

The Northern Territory's second biggest population centre has more than 24,000 inhabitants. When it comes to climate, they are extremists. In the summer it gets as hot as 42 °C (107 °F) but, mercifully, the nights in June, July and August require a sweater or two. Chances of seeing rain are slight. The Henley-on-Todd Regatta, a whimsical fixture each August, is run on the sandy bed of the sometime Todd river, a wide wadi gullying through the centre of town. The boats, of many classes, are all bottomless, hilariously propelled by the racing legs of their crews.

"The Alice" first grew around a waterhole discovered in 1871 by the surveying party stringing the first telegraph line from Adelaide to Darwin—and from there to the rest of the world. Alice Springs was named after Alice Todd, the wife of South Australia's Postmaster General. He won a knighthood for pushing through the project; locally, the Todd River immortalizes him.

Camels, traditionally jockeyed by experts from Afghanistan, brought the equipment for the telegraph relay station built at Alice Springs and the supplies to keep the technicians alive. When the termites devoured the first telegraph poles, replacements—heavy iron poles manufactured in Britain—also had to be transported by camel train.

Telegrams aside, Alice Springs remained isolated until World War II. And until the 1960s it was little more than a crossroads market town. Now it's thriving as a staging post for tourist jaunts throughout the Red Centre.

Like many an Australian town, "the Alice" is bigger in area than you might expect, but the essential atmosphere can be taken in on a walking tour. In the main street, **Todd Street,** you'll find the Northern Territory Government Tourist Bureau, with maps and brochures. Nearby are historic buildings like the **Old Stuart Town Gaol** from the beginning of the 20th century, with "his" and "hers" dormitory cells, and **Adelaide House,** the first hospital, now a museum.

Panorama "Guth" on Hartley Street is the realization of a dream by a Dutch artist, Henk Guth—a monumental panoramic painting of the local landscape,

Aspects of Alice life transform a drab wall.

Improvised seating for the Alice Springs Camel Derby.

60 metres (200 feet) in circumference. Downstairs is a museum of outstanding Aboriginal art and artefacts.

The **Flying Doctor Service,** which brings health care to the farthest cattle ranch, began here in 1928. You can take a tour of the base, on the south side of town. Another service which eased development of the Outback, the **School of the Air,** a radio link with isolated pupils, is headquartered on Head Street.

A couple of kilometres north of town, an unspoiled park surrounds the restored **Telegraph Station.** This was the most important relay station on the line. Before the wires were strung a message could take three months to reach London from

from a kneeling start in a cloud of dust, run as fast as race-horses, though less gracefully.

You may be surprised to find that a town like Alice has an "international standard" **casino.** Seven nights a week, until 1 a.m., enthusiasts have a choice of blackjack, roulette and a sophisticated version of the Australian game of two-up (see p. 138), along with the excitements of poker machines and keno, a game resembling bingo.

An eccentric enterprise southeast of town is a desert winery. **Chateau Hornsby** produces about 25 tons of grapes per year. In this hostile climate the vines have to be irrigated daily. The resulting wines, with quaint names like Alice Springs Shiraz and The Ghan Moselle, may be sampled on the spot.

A popular excursion from "the Alice" concentrates on **Standley Chasm,** 50 kilometres (30 miles) to the west. This passage through the MacDonnell Ranges dwindles to the narrowest gap. The walls are so high and steep that the sun penetrates the bottom only fleetingly at midday. Slender trees bravely sprout from the rockface high above, reflected in the cool, still water of a natural pool at the far end of the gorge. In the "wet" season, from November to March, rainwater can suddenly flood the chasm.

Adelaide. The relics here give a glimpse of 19th-century technology and the lonely life of the telegraph pioneers.

South of "the Alice" on the Ross Highway, a **camel farm** offers rides atop swaying beasts, the descendants of the camels that supplied the pioneers. Every May the local Lions Club sponsors the Camel Cup, a day of camel races at Blatherskite Park. The animals, launched

111

AYERS ROCK

As the sun begins to sink beyond the rim of the desert, the crowds with their cameras gather by car and bus along "Sunset Strip", the tongue-in-cheek name for a dusty stretch of parking lot. Watching Ayers Rock undergo its striking changes of colour, the onlookers are not solemn but rather festive, friendly and relaxed ... in fact, very Australian. They are fulfilling an Australian dream, getting to know this mystical, 500-million-year-old rock that rises from the red heart of the country.

The world's greatest rock, seemingly dropped by divine design in the middle of nowhere, actually protrudes from a buried mountain range. About 350 metres (1,150 feet) high and some 8 kilometres (5 miles) around, it is even more impres-

Pickets and chain mark out the long steep haul to the top of Ayers Rock.

Open Wide, Please

Australia's most spectacular lizard, found in the northern desert, is an exhibitionist called Chlamydosaurus kingii. If it's courting, or generally under stress or feeling imperilled, the frilled lizard unveils its secret weapon: it opens wide its mouth, and around it, a big swath of skin unfurls like an umbrella. This speckled frill opens as wide as a magazine. Standing on its hind legs, the lizard rocks menacingly from side to side. By way of sound effects it expels a scary hiss. If all that doesn't work, it can attack with a lash of its tail. Or run quickly from the battlefield.

Australia counts hundreds of species of lizard, none, happily, venomous. The same cannot be said about the slithery range of snakes available.

112

sive than the dimensions suggest. Standing alone in a landscape as flat as the floor, and tinted as bright as your imagination, the monolith lives up to its reputation. You'll need no complicated explanations to understand why the Aborigines consider it sacred.

The Aborigines have owned Ayers Rock (they call it Uluru) under Australian law only since 1985; the small local Aboriginal community leases it back to the government for use as a national park, in return for a healthy income and participation in its management. The handover of the land created a raging controversy; vociferous opponents advertised the slogan, "The rock belongs to *all* Australians."

For the Aborigines it's not just a rock, it's a vital aspect of

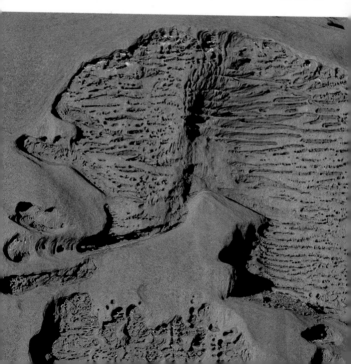

Dreamtime, encompassing the creation of the earth, linked with the life of the present and future. Various parts of the monolith are qualified as sacred sites; they are signposted, fenced off, and definitely barred to outsiders.

The most inspiring views of the rock are to be seen at dawn and dusk. It's worth getting up at six in the morning to stake out the mighty silhouette from

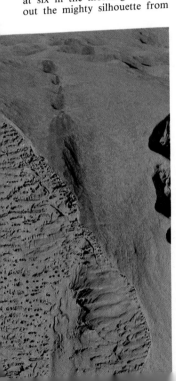

20 kilometres away, waiting for the sunrise. As first light strikes the lonely monolith it catches fire, glowing red, then orange, finally seeming to emit rays of wondrous power. Only then the desert world comes to life: a hawk squawks, a rabbit rustles the brush, and hordes of pesky flies begin to buzz. Waving your hand in front of your face soon becomes second nature in the Outback, like a horse flicking its tail. Insect repellent helps, too, but the flies seem to outnumber the people 20 to one. Maybe this is why Aboriginal legends mention bothersome flies.

After breakfast you can join the crowds climbing the rock. A few hours suffice for the round-trip via the marked trail, which has a protective chain to grab when the going gets too steep or windy. The ascent requires no mountain-climbing experience or equipment. But do wear sensible rubber-soled shoes and carry drinking water. From ground level the climbers attaining the summit look like a line of very tired ants. Another worthwhile way to get to know the rock is to join a walking tour led by a park ranger, circumnavigating the base. Up close, the monolith

Every scratch, cleft and asperity on Uluru has a symbolic meaning.

115

discloses its variegated surface: caves, dry rivulets, furrows and burrows, wounds and gashes, and what might be taken for fanciful engravings 60 metres (200 feet) tall.

Only 36 kilometres (22 miles) by road west of Ayers Rock, and visible from its summit, is another stupendous rock formation, the **Olgas.** From afar, Mount Olga and its satellites look like a scattering of dinosaur eggs or sleeping elephants, but they're even higher than Ayers Rock. Here, too, dawn and dusk colour the most fascinating views, the fantasy shapes changing with the hues and the movement of the shadows. You can get to know the Olgas by a choice of hiking routes. The popular trail from the Katatjuta car park up to the lookout is officially called "suitable for family enjoyment", but it's steep and tricky enough to deter the very youngest and oldest generations.

Yulara Development

To cope with hundreds of thousands of visitors each year at Ayers Rock, a comprehensive resort has been built. It could have been a disastrous blot on the landscape, but the **Yulara Resort**

In the desert west of Yulara, clumps of spinifex echo the contours of the Olgas.

117

fits in benignly, 20 kilometres (12 miles) from the rock. Almost camouflaged, the complex is too low-slung to detract from the majesty of the surroundings.

The facilities start with hundreds of sites for tents and caravans, and go up to a five-star hotel with gardens, pool, spa, restaurants and bars, television and in-house video; and of course all the rooms are air-conditioned. It makes for quite a change after a day slogging through the desert. The permanent party running Yulara amounts to about 500 people, recruited in many parts of the country. There is a school for their children and local Aboriginal children. In other resorts the staff quarters tend to be hidden from sight, but they are so luxurious at Yulara that they're set in the midst of the prime tourist area.

The **Visitors' Centre** in the hotel-and-shopping complex offers information, literature and audiovisual shows explaining the desert, the wildlife, geology, mythology, and other angles to enhance your appreciation of the Red Centre.

Several airlines serve Yulara, and the views of the desert on the way are spellbinding. Otherwise you can take a bus or drive; it's about 450 kilometres (360 miles) by paved road from Alice Springs, a whole day to become acquainted with the desert in its many forms—flat and desolate, or covered with scrub, thinly forested or, more rarely, sand undulating in postcard-worthy dunes.

The best time of year to visit is between May and October, when the days are sunny and warm and the nights refreshingly chill. In January, by contrast, the mean maximum temperature is 36.6 °C (98 °F), not quite conducive to hiking.

Kindly Juggernauts

First there was a trailer-truck, then a trailer-truck with a caboose. In the Northern Territory the idea was taken to its limit: the road train. A mighty truck pulling two or three full-sized trailers can measure 50 metres (165 feet) from headlight to tail. It's marked "road train" front and rear to warn you that this is no ordinary vehicle.

If you're driving behind a road train, trying to overtake requires patience, good driving skills, strong nerves, and at least one kilometre of empty road ahead. Fortunately, road train drivers are courteous professionals who'll give you a fair chance. In exchange, they ask you to understand that their momentum makes sudden manoeuvres very dangerous. If somebody has to give way, it had better be you.

FOR THE FEARLESS: SURVIVING THE NEVER-NEVER

Three-quarters of Australia is desert—"burning wastes of barren soil and sand", as Henry Lawson described it. These vast empty spaces on the map hold an irresistible challenge for intrepid adventurers. Only vaguely comparable with desert of the Sahara type, the far Outback supports vegetation—sometimes even luxuriant—and fascinating wildlife. If you do want to venture off the surfaced roads and explore the unknown, you must take a few precautions.

● Do not even consider driving into the Outback in the summer: the heat is unbearable. In the 1840s, explorer Charles Sturt recorded temperatures of 157 °F (69.5 °C) in the open and 132 °C (55.5 °C) in the shade. It was hot enough to melt the lead in his pencil and force screws out of wooden boxes. Just think what it could do to your car.

● Rain can also be a source of disaster: after many years of drought, it can suddenly pour down for a week, and the land is transformed into an enormous flood plain. Never camp in a dry river bed.

● Your vehicle should be a reliable four-wheel-drive, with a complete set of spare parts: two spare tyres and tyre repair kit, two spare tubes, coil, condenser, fan belt, radiator hoses and distributor points, a tin of radiator leak fixative, spark plugs, an extra jack (with a large baseplate to prevent sinking in sand or mud), 5 litres of engine oil, a pump, a tool-kit, an axe and a small shovel. Keep the petrol tank full and carry at least 20 litres in reserve.

● You will need reliable maps, and you should plan your route in detail—and stick to the plan relentlessly. At your point of departure, advise the police of your route, the estimated time of arrival at destination, and the amount of rations you are carrying. Report to the police again when you arrive. Always seek local advice about the hazards you may encounter. If you wish to enter Aboriginal lands, you must obtain permission from the Aboriginal landowners, and at least four weeks' notice is required. Enquire at the government tourist office for the appropriate address. In some areas you have to be equipped with two-way radio.

● Take adequate supplies. Most important is water—you will need 6 litres per person per day, best carried in metal containers. Emergency rations should consist of high energy foods such as dried fruit, with canned meats, soup and fruit drinks. Invaluable components of your first-aid kit are aspirin, water-purifying tablets, salt tablets, diarrhoea pills, insect repellent, disinfectant, bandages and sun-block cream. Your personal survival kit, to be carried on your person at all times, should contain a compass, map, whistle, waterproof matches, pocket-knife, bandage and sticking plaster.

● Other essentials: a set of billy-cans, several sheets of heavy-duty plastic, 2 metres square, and a length of rubber or plastic tubing. A piece of nylon rope (30 metres long) may also be useful.

● Wear loose, light cotton clothing and cover your head. Space blankets can prove a boon: the shiny aluminium side turned towards the sun reflects heat away from the body, keeping the temperature normal. To keep warm, turn the shiny side inwards.

● Do not drive at night. Kangaroos are a real hazard, and you may collide with cattle, which are attracted to the roads at night because the surface is warmer than the ground itself.

In Case of Catastrophe

If your car breaks down—above all do not panic. Stay with your vehicle: it will be a welcome source of shade, and it is more easily spotted by aircraft.

● Make visible distress signals, using brightly coloured clothing, bedding or any other available material—anything that contrasts strongly with the earth.

● Move as little as possible, to conserve body fluid—all physical exertion should take place during the cool night hours.

● Your main preoccupation must be water. Ration your supply, and set about collecting more by making a solar still. Dig a hole about 1 metre square and 50 centimetres deep, away from any shade. Place a large billycan in the bottom of the hole, and surround it with leafy foliage. Cover the hole with a sheet of plastic and seal the edges completely with earth, making sure that the plastic does not touch the interior walls of the hole. If you have a length of rubber or plastic tubing, place it in the bottom of the billycan before you seal the edges of the sheeting, leaving the other end outside to act as a siphon. Place a small stone in the centre of the plastic sheet, right over the billycan. Moisture from the ground will condense on the underside of the plastic sheet and will drip slowly into the billycan. In this way you will collect about 2 litres of water per hole per day, so it's best to make several stills, at least 3 metres apart. You will need to change the position of the still every three to four days.

● Small animals—frogs, lizards and snakes—are attracted to the stills and may provide an extra source of food. In principle, anything that walks, crawls, swims, flies or grows from the soil is edible—or so they say. But beware of anything with a bitter taste and plants with a milky sap.

● Another source of food and water in the north-west of Australia is the bottle tree, which preserves water in its hollow trunk for months after the wet season. In an emergency you can also eat the rind of bottle tree pods, chopped up and stirred with water—nourishing but certainly not gourmet fare.

The prospects may seem harrowing—but after all, the Aborigines have survived this forbidding land for 40,000 years.

The water splash is a seasonal hazard—most of the year it's as dry as dust.

WESTERN AUSTRALIA

When it comes to elbow room, the state of Western Australia has no competition. It's a Texas sort of place, though bigger than Texas and Alaska combined, and more than ten times the area of Great Britain.

Most of its vast expanse is desert, semidesert or otherwise difficult if not impossible terrain. So the bulk of the population of 1¼ million has gravitated to the Mediterranean climate around the beautiful capital city, Perth. Closer to Jakarta than to Sydney, Perth faces the Indian Ocean with an open, outward-looking stance. The cares of the big population centres of eastern Australia seem worlds away.

The state's Outback produces great wealth, even the forbidding deserts bursting with minerals. Gold brought the first bonanza, in the 1880s and '90s, followed by nickel, bauxite and iron.

Much more appealing are the visible riches: the hardwood forests, orchards and vineyards. And, since the climate is so sunny, it's only fair that there's a beach for every mood along the 6,400 kilometres (4,000 miles) of coastline.

The first European to set eyes on a Western Australian beach (in 1616) was Dirk Hartog, a Dutch navigator making his way from the Cape of Good Hope to Java. Soon, other Dutch travellers touched base, and one of them reported spotting a wallaby, though not by name; he thought it was a giant cat with a pouch for its kitten. Later in the 17th century, the British adventurer William Dampier happened upon Shark Bay, near Carnarvon, and could hardly wait to leave: the land seemed hopeless for farming, there was no drinking water, and he dismissed the Aborigines as "brutes".

More than 200 years after Hartog's discovery of Western Australia, the British finally got around to colonizing it. The site chosen, on the Swan River, became Perth. But what the Co-

The Circular Pool in the Hamersley Ranges—a green oasis in the Western wild.

It seldom rains in Perth. And even when it does, the "city of lights" glows from within.

lonial Office considered a good idea turned out to be less brilliant in practice. It would take more than the scenery and climate to attract settlers to what seemed, even by Australian standards, the end of the world. Problems of development persisted: poor communications, financial difficulties, and a shortage of workers. Prospects for the new frontier became so precarious that the colony's leaders had to appeal to London to send out forced labourers—convicts.

Still nothing really worked in Western Australia until the gold rush toward the end of the 19th century. Then the population quadrupled in ten years. Once

PERTH

Brimming with vigour and optimism, bright new high-rise office buildings scrape the clear blue skies of Perth. If this city were a person, you might imagine it had been born with a silver spoon in its mouth: a handsome, cleancut youngster with every possible advantage, inevitably growing up to become an unqualified success in life.

Although history refutes the silver spoon theory, you can't miss Perth's easy self-confidence. The people are relaxed, friendly, anxious to help the stranger. They are proud of their efficient town and its up-to-date facilities—the shopping arcades, the bus service, the art galleries and Entertainment Centre—and the great sailing, swimming, surfing and fishing on the doorstep. They won't fail to inform you that this tidy city sprawling magnificently along the looping river is Australia's sunniest state capital.

Sunshine aside, Perth has called itself "the city of lights" since the early days of the American manned space programme. As John Glenn, the first American to orbit the earth, passed overhead, middle-of-the-night Perth switched on every light bulb in town. It was a friendly gesture, brightening the lone astronaut's flight and putting Perth's name in lights.

launched on the road to prosperity, there was no stopping the largest state. Its isolation finally ended in the early years of the 20th century when the transcontinental railway linked Perth and Sydney. Western Australia reached new heights of self-confidence and fame in 1983, when the yacht *Australia II* wrested the America's Cup from the U.S. for the first time in 132 years.

City Sights

Few get a chance to enjoy a spaceman's perspective, but the view over Perth from **King's Park** is a good compromise for sizing up the city below. These 400 hectares (1,000 acres) of natural woodland and wild flowers, manicured lawns and picnic sites, solemn monuments and lively playgrounds, occupy the top of a bluff called Mount Eliza, right on the edge of the city centre. From here you look down on the wide Swan River as it meanders towards the sea, the business district with its gleaming skyscrapers, and the complexity of the well-landscaped municipal freeway system.

The **Swan River** was named after the indigenous black swans, first noted with amazement by the 17th-century Dutch navigator Willem de Vlaming. Unlike northern hemisphere swans, which are white and prone to whistling or grunting when they are not naturally mute, the blacks sound off like a band of clarinets noisily tuning up. They're so tame they'll take bread out of the palm of your hand without biting.

The Swan River begins about 240 kilometres (150 miles) inland in the wheatlands of Western Australia. For most of its journey, under the name of the Avon River, it is only seasonally navigable, and occasionally downright treacherous. But here, with the Indian Ocean close enough to salt it, the Swan widens into a lake, and invites reflection ... and flotillas of breezy sailing boats.

Near the riverside in the centre of town, the **Old Courthouse** really is old, especially by local standards. Built in Georgian style in 1836, it qualifies as the oldest public building in Perth.

A step back in time in Perth's shopping district.

126

Stirling Gardens, surrounding the courthouse, is a restful hideaway. A monument here looks like a giant shish kebab impaling all of the minerals produced in Western Australia; but don't expect to find gold or diamonds on the skewer—they don't seem to count.

Town Hall, at the corner of Hay and Barrack Streets, was built in the 1860s by convict labour. If you look closely at the outline of the windows of the tower, you may perceive the design of broad arrows—the prison symbol that was stencilled on convicts' uniforms.

Similarly Tudor in inspiration, but even less antique than the Town Hall, **London Court** is a 1930s shopping mall done up in 16th-century style, leaded windows and all. It fits in quite happily with the modern stores and interconnecting shopping precincts radiating from the **Hay Street Mall,** the main shopping street of Perth. Cars are prohibited here, so the window-shopping is very relaxed. The mall is usually animated by buskers—street musicians, magicians, jugglers or mimes—and fast-talking pedlars.

A short walk westwards, in the busy traffic-choked part of Hay

Primitive art for newfangled music: eye-catching entrance to a Perth nightclub.

Street, the state **tourist office,** called the Holiday WA Centre, is an abundant source of brochures, maps, tickets, tours and bright ideas cheerfully dispensed.

In a city as young as Perth, with a skyline of tall, modern office buildings, the historic structures which have escaped the developer's demolition ball are proudly pointed out to visitors.

Government House, on the main street, St. George's Terrace, is the official residence of the state governor. Its Gothic effects date from the 1860s. Built by convicts, the house is used nowadays for state occasions and as a place to put up visiting VIPs.

The elegant terrace leads straight to the **Barracks Archway,** the last vestige of a headquarters building of the 1860s. This crenellated three-storey structure has been preserved as a memorial to the early colonists. Behind the brick archway you can see **Parliament House,** where the state legislature holds forth.

On the other side of the railway tracks—you can cross the unusual Horseshoe Bridge by foot or car—stands the **Old Gaol,** built by and for convicts in 1856. Now it's part of the **Western Australia Museum.** In addition to penal relics of the wild west days, the museum contains a good collection of Aboriginal rock paintings, headdresses and weapons, as well as a meteorite

129

weighing in at 11 tons. The **Western Australia Art Gallery,** close by, exhibits paintings from several continents.

Also north of the city centre is the **Northbridge** district, full of restaurants of many nationalities, pubs and nightclubs, ample proof that there is indeed life after dark in Perth. Alternatively, under one roof, **Burswood Casino,** near the Causeway Bridge, has more than 140 gaming tables, plus a cabaret, restaurants and bars.

Back in the centre of town, you can hardly miss the modern **Entertainment Centre.** Not quite Perth's answer to the Sydney Opera House, this roundhouse landmark can pack in 8,000 fans for rock stars or ballet. Another cultural focus is the **Concert Hall,** headquarters of the state's symphony orchestra. And for stage plays, the most atmospheric house is **His Majesty's Theatre,** restored to its sumptuous Edwardian standard.

TO THE COAST

It's only 19 kilometres (13 miles) down the river from Perth to the capital's Indian Ocean port, Fremantle—an enjoyable outing on one of the cruise boats that ply the **Swan River.**

The river tours begin in the centre of Perth, at the Barrack Street Jetty. On the south side of the Narrows Bridge, note the **Old Mill,** an imposing white windmill in the Dutch style, from the first half of the 19th century. Perfectly restored, it's open for visits, but check the limited schedule.

Beyond this, on the opposite shore, spreads what looks like another transplant from Europe. The campus of the **University of Western Australia** was built and landscaped in Mediterranean style, from the shrubs right up to the orange-tiled roofs.

Matilda Bay harbours only a relative handful of the swarms of sailing boats calling the Swan River home. During World War II this was a base for Catalina flying boats. The bay is the site of the Royal Perth Yacht Club, where the America's Cup was treasured behind bullet-proof glass from 1983 until it was lost to the United States in 1987.

The coastline of the **Dalkeith** district, near Point Resolution, is reasonably enough called Millionaires' Row. The view of these mansions from the river perspective just might evoke a dash of envy; even millionaires from out of town could turn jealous. The guided tour commentary goes on at great length about the cost of the houses, the fame of their owners, and the foibles of the owners' private lives.

Freshwater Bay was named by the crew of *HMS Beagle,* the survey ship made famous as the vehicle for Charles Darwin's researches into nature. After this bay, and a zig and a zag, the river tapers to a relatively narrow-gauge artery crossed by two bridges. Long-suffering convict labour built the first bridge at this site in 1866. It proved a boon to one of its creators, a celebrated outlaw named Moondyne Joe, an escape artist. The night before the ribbon-cutting ceremony, he broke out of Fremantle Prison and gave himself the honour of becoming the first, if unofficial, pedestrian to cross the Bridge Over the River Swan. He made a clean getaway.

Fremantle

Although it's a serious international port for passengers and cargo, you'll remember the city of Fremantle for its casual charms. A Mediterranean-style sunniness combines with Victorian quaintness to give Fremantle a special character. The town is cosmopolitan, yet as down-to-earth as its classic examples of convict architecture.

For years Fremantle—Freo to abbreviation-prone Aussies—lay becalmed, a long way from the big time of tourism. Then came the America's Cup saga and a saturation of world attention. New pride inspired the townsfolk in a sparkling campaign to restore the old terraced houses and

other relics in time for the 1986/87 defence of the Cup. At the same time, the marina facilities were vastly expanded.

Whether you think of Fremantle as a yachting base or a workaday port, you'll want to see the sights of the harbour. There are dream yachts, trawlers, ocean liners and cargo ships of every stripe. You may see one of them, a special sheep ship, loading tens of thousands of sheep from all over Western Australia, bound for the Middle East. Dogs help the shepherds direct truckloads of reluctant "passengers" to their berths. The sheep live on pellets of food for the four-week journey.

Fremantle's highest point is **Monument Hill**, in War Memorial Park. There are three memorials here, including one for the U.S. personnel based in Fremantle who died in World War II. Another, an actual periscope, commemorates the British and Allied submarine crews who perished in the same conflict. This is the place to watch the sun set over the Indian Ocean.

Back near the waterfront, and wasting an enviable view, the 12-sided **Round House** looks like the forbidding, windowless prison it used to be. Actually it's much more cheerful from the inside, with its sunny courtyard. Built in 1831, the Round House specialized in the lesser crimi-

131

nals, although it was the site of the state's first hanging; generally, incorrigibles were shipped off to the rigours of Tasmania.

The **Western Australian Maritime Museum** was built by convicts to house the Commissariat, the bureaucracy in charge of them. Here's a chance to see some shipwrecks, most notably the wooden hull of the 600-ton *Batavia,* flagship of the Dutch East India Company, which went aground in 1629. Meticulous restoration work is under way to reassemble this rare example of 17th-century shipbuilding technology.

A wide-open space beyond the Maritime Museum, the **Esplanade** is shaded by Norfolk pines and a sprawling Moreton Bay fig tree. A monument here immortalizes Captain Charles Fremantle, who in 1829 claimed for Britain the west coast of what was then New Holland.

The **Fremantle Museum and Arts Centre,** at the other end of town, occupies yet another convict-built complex. It first served as an asylum for deranged prisoners, then a training centre for midwives, later an old women's home, and in World War II it found new life as a headquarters of the U.S. Navy. Demobilized and brightly restored, the Colonial Gothic building now houses exhibits on the history of Fremantle and its people.

Rottnest Island

Don't be put off by the name: there is nothing rotten in the state of Western Australia, and certainly not on Rottnest Island. Even in the original Dutch, the name does the island no justice. It seems that Commodore Willem de Vlaming, who landed here in 1696, confused the indigenous quokkas (a sort of undersized wallaby) with some imaginary

---

Blazing Flowers

Every springtime, as early as August, the roadsides and fields of Western Australia break out in colour as the wild flowers bloom. Even the deserts are transformed into flower gardens for the occasion. Thousands of different species spring up overnight. The big show continues until about October, in all the shades of the spectrum.

Because of Western Australia's isolation, most of the flowering plants are found nowhere else. So flower-lovers from all over the continent and abroad flock to see exhibits as vivid as the green and red kangaroo paw, the official floral emblem of the state.

Among the best places to enjoy spectacular displays are Yanchep National Park and the jarrah forests of the south-west. Or you can stay in Perth and see the blooming miracle in miniature in King's Park.

---

species of rat. So he called the island Rottnest, or rat's nest. In spite of this unkind mistake, the Dutch explorer considered Rottnest an earthly paradise. You'll probably agree.

A good reason for going over the sea to Rottnest (18 kilometres or 12 miles from Fremantle) is to see the fetching little quokkas, with babies in the pouch like their kangaroo cousins. These friendly marsupials accept hand-outs from visitors. Other attractions are peacocks and pheasants, which were introduced when the governors of Western Australia used the island as a summer residence. And you can spot dozens of other species of birds, like

Beaufortia decussata—or gravel bottlebrush—blooms only in Western Australia.

the curlew sandpiper, the red-necked stint and the osprey. Since 1941 the island has been a wildlife sanctuary, where it's forbidden to tamper with all of nature, even the snakes.

Rottnest is as quiet as an idyllic, barefoot sort of isle ought to be. The number of cars is severely curtailed, and skateboards are emphatically banned. Bicycles are the most popular way of exploring the 40 kilometres (25 miles) of coastline. Look into the swimming, snorkelling, fishing and boating.

The island can be reached from Perth by commuter plane, ferryboat or hydrofoil.

EXCURSIONS INLAND
Just east of Perth, the **Darling Range** is the beginning of the great inland plateau. Amidst the tall trees and wild flowers are lookout points for views of the city and the sea. Waterfalls, brooks and dams refresh the relaxing scene.

A man-made natural attraction in the Darling Range, **El Caballo Blanco** ("the white horse" in Spanish) is the comfortable home from home of a troupe of Andalusian dancing horses. Tours take in the stables and pastures, followed by a performance starring the superbly trained white steeds.

The **Swan Valley,** only about half an hour's drive north-east of Perth, is a high priority destination for wine-lovers. The area is noted for its small, family-run vineyards, which produce red and white wines and fortified dessert wines. The wine-making

Sentinels in a moonscape, the Pinnacles cast unearthly shadows.

tradition in the Swan Valley dates back to the very foundation of Western Australia. If wine tasting and driving seem incompatible, you can take a coach tour of selected vineyards, or even a river cruise with stops at one or two wine cellars.

Farther east, the green expanse of the **Avon Valley** provides pasture land for cattle and grows the grain to feed Perth and beyond.

The colony's first inland settlement, **York** is proud of its history. More than a dozen 19th-century buildings have been restored; several now serve as museums. Just outside town, one of the early farms has been restored to a "living museum" in which you can watch blacksmiths and wheelwrights at work. Clydesdale horses still plough the fields.

The nearest national park to Perth, **Yanchep**, is known for its eucalyptus forests, wild flowers and series of limestone caves. There is also an island-studded lake called Loch McNess, named after a local philanthropist, Sir Charles McNess. Don't bother looking for a Loch McNess monster. But you can see a koala colony. Along the ocean, **Atlantis Marine Park** features performing seals and dolphins, and intrepid employees hand-feed sharks and stingrays.

Natural Wonders

A spectacle reckoned to be more than 2½ billion years old, **Wave Rock** is one of those natural phenomena worth a long detour. It's near the small town of Hyden, about 350 kilometres (220 miles) inland from Perth, in the wide open spaces where the wheat, oats and barley grow. The rock itself takes the form of a stupendous surfer's wave, as tall as a five-storey building, eternally on the verge of breaking. Walking under the impending splash is one of the state's most popular tourist activities. Energetic visitors can also climb to the top. A wildlife sanctuary and a golf course complete the attractions here. Other extraordinary rock formations in the area have expressive names like Hippo's Yawn and The Humps.

In **Nambung National Park**, about 250 kilometres (155 miles) north of Perth, the rocky marvels take the form of myriad limestone pillars jutting like stalagmites from the desert floor. Standing as high as 5 or 6 metres (16 to 20 feet), the **Pinnacles** are scattered over perhaps a thousand acres. The imagination runs wild. The park entrance is near the lobstering village of Cervantes.

The South-West

Excursions to the south-western corner of the state encompass a delightful variety of scenery: beaches, vineyards, orchards and soaring **jarrah forests.** Where the water table is high, you'll see stands of paperbark trees; you could strip off a layer of the papyrus-style bark and write a letter. But the most impressive tree in the region is the jarrah, a giant variety of eucalyptus. The lower half grows straight and clean as a telephone pole, with all the branches emerging at the top.

One of the curiosities of the region is its underground wealth. This is bauxite country; so much of the mineral (vital in the production of aluminium) occurs here that the leftovers are used in the surfacing of the roads. The bauxite is transported along "the world's longest conveyor belt", about 50 kilometres (more than 30 miles) long. The belt, which crosses the "aluminium-paved" roads, is as much a part of the forest scenery as the lumbermen's trucks.

Bus tours also visit the Muja open-cast coal mine, not quite the sort of view you might have expected, but remarkable by any standard. At the end of a shift you can watch the ballet performed by dozens of ore-carrying behemoths, their movements tightly coordinated as they converge on the parking lots.

THE GOLDFIELDS

The Golden Mile, where fortunes were made and lost overnight, may not inspire flights of poetry. There's nary a tree, just desert and scrub, dilapidated shacks, and the skeletons of mining superstructures. You'd hardly guess, but the goldfields of Western Australia are still booming, thanks to new technology and deeper digs.

Kalgoorlie, about 550 air kilometres (340 miles) east of Perth,

The Emu is Grounded

If emus had complexes, they might feel insecure about not knowing how to fly. It's the sort of problem that made the dodo extinct. Another embarrassment: the emu is only the second biggest bird in the world, the African ostrich taking first prize. Still, some emu males stand as tall as a man, which is rather impressive for an ungainly character all in feather.

You have to give credit to the male emu's sense of family responsibility. While the young mother is off gallivanting, the father guards the eggs and then looks after the chicks until they can face life on their own. They are born with camouflage stripes, helping to keep them inconspicuous in grassland.

Like the ostrich, the emu's pop-eyed face gives little sign of intelligence. But if it's in a rush, the emu is smart enough to run at 50 kilometres an hour or more.

Two-Up in the Bush

The Kalgoorlie Two-Up School may sound like a kindergarten, but you must be 18 years old to enter the ramshackle arena. Signposted as a tourist attraction, this gambling den resembles a cockfight ring in some obscure Latin country.

The rules of the game, invented by old-time convicts, could hardly be simpler. The ringkeeper appoints one of the players as "spinner", to toss two pennies. The spinner's goal is to toss two heads. Most of the betting on his chances of success takes place "on the side", informally, between customers. Scrupulous honesty reigns, and verbal bets are considered debts of honour.

Bets range from $10 to a car or house. The game goes on daily except once a fortnight—miners' payday. By popular demand of the miners' wives.

retains the atmosphere of the riotous gold-rush town it was in the 1890s. The streets, laid out in a grid, are wide enough for stagecoaches or camel trains to U-turn. Like a Wild West movie set, there are verandahed saloons for every occasion. A pawnbroker's window displays a used metal detector—a short, sad story of failure. But if this doesn't discourage you, join the optimists scanning old worked-over sites

in search of forgotten nuggets. The occasional whopper still turns up.

The first big strike of Kalgoorlie gold came in June, 1893, when an Irishman, Patrick Hannan, stumbled onto enough glitter to shout about. Paddy Hannan has never been forgotten in Kalgoorlie. A bronze statue of the bearded prospector adorns the main street, which bears his name; the water bag he carries

138

In Kalgoorlie's main street, townsfolk anticipate a political demonstration.

serves as the municipal water fountain.

The almost total lack of water was the first desperate hardship to face the thousands of prospectors who rushed into the goldfields when Hannan's news spread. Disease and death by dehydration took a heavy toll. The solution was found by an Irish engineer C.Y. O'Connor, who built a 560-kilometre (350-mile) pipeline from a reservoir near Perth. You can still see the big above-ground pipes along the road. Wounded by criticism of the project, O'Connor killed himself before the first drop of water reached Kalgoorlie; he is honoured by a statue on the seafront in Fremantle.

As the prospectors came in

139

from the surrounding desert with their sudden wealth, Kalgoorlie became a rip-roaring supplier of wine, women and song. The pubs were legion; many retain their frontier atmosphere. Another old mining tradition is the red-light district of Hay Street, where the camp-followers are on display to this day, in the window-seat manner of Amsterdam. As for gambling, the town doesn't have a casino, but a few kilometres out in the country "Australia's only legalized bush two-up school" flourishes from midday to sundown.

In the centre of the Golden Mile, the **Hainault Gold Mine** has taken on a new lease of life as an underground monument. Three or four times a day, seven days a week, retired miners take tour groups down to the depths in a claustrophobic cage to show how the seams were blasted and the gold extracted. The Hainault Mine earned its place in history. From 1920 to 1947 alone it produced 35 tons of gold.

Coolgardie, 40 kilometres (25 miles) west of Kalgoorlie, proudly bears the slogan of "ghost town". In fact, ghosting is its principal industry, and if there's a bit of melancholy in the air, it must be good for business. The historical markers seem to outnumber the population.

Gold was discovered at Coolgardie a year before Paddy Hannan's big strike at Kalgoorlie. By the turn of the century Coolgardie's population was 15,000. You can see how prosperous the town was from the elegance of the Victorian buildings, most notably the three-storey arcaded headquarters of the **Goldfields Museum.** This institution is stacked with exhibits detailing the difficult life and work of the prospectors.

Any good ghost town needs an interesting cemetery, and the inscriptions on the headstones in Coolgardie's graveyard tell revealing stories of the harsh frontier life. Among the Afghani camel drivers buried here, one is listed as the victim of a murder.

KIMBERLEYS

More than 15 hundred kilometres north of the gold lode, one of the world's richest diamond mines gives a sparkle to the rugged, remote Kimberley region of Western Australia.

The Argyle mine produces a sizeable heap of exquisite pink diamonds—a coveted rarity in the gem world—as well as vast quantities of industrial diamonds, used for grinding and drilling. Machines beside which mere humans look like Lilliputians move the ore to the Argyle processing plant, where millions of carats per year are yielded. This otherwise inhospitable area is thought to hide

SOUTH AUSTRALIA

The history of South Australia is distinctive. Nothing so gross as convict settlers here; the colony was founded as a planned community run by wealthy idealists. The "free settlers only" tag is a source of local pride. Sobriet' and morality were keystones the master plan, giving rise t reputation of stuffy puritan But in relatively recent the influence of the "wo (bluenoses or killjoys) ha For example, Australi ists legally conquered beach just outside Ad

Spread out acros square kilometres (3 miles), South Aus one-eighth of the But, most of th endurable dese number only of Australia' these may tentedly i city, Ade

ADE

With
airp
cie
A
t

squares and broad

...ion is less

is a

the
bo

WESTERN AUSTRALIA

Before the diamond boom, the modern tropical town of **Kununurra** (an Aboriginal word meaning, appropriately, "big waters") was best known as a dam site. It's the centre of the far-reaching Ord River Scheme. Diversion Dam has changed the character of the region, bottling the monsoon-flooded river and distributing the water for irrigation purposes in the dry season.

as much as half of all the diamonds on earth.

The astonishing potential of the Argyle diamond field, 120 kilometres (75 miles) from the nearest town, Kununurra, wasn't discovered until 1979. Full-scale production began in 1985.

A spectre of desolation still haunts the ghost town of Coolgardie.

The project created Lake Argyle, which contains nine times as much water as Sydney Harbour. A holiday village overlooki[ng] this, the country's biggest re[ser]voir, is a centre for swimm[ing,] fishing, boating and hike[s.] best season is from May [to Sep]tember, when the days a[re warm] and the nights comforta[ble.]

The West Kimberl[ey yields] precious stones, too—[notably] the Argyle diam[onds.] These great rocks [could] be a couple of b[illion years?] rate among the [most an]cient geological [formations?] and gorges p[rovide?] along the F[itzroy?] either rippl[e?] on the sea[?]

The se[?] romanti[c?] 80 pe[r?] moth[er?] Japa[nese?] pin[?] in[?]

144

B[?]
pearl b[?]
drain with t[?]
cultured pearls a[?]
tons. Broome's China[town?] old Japanese boarding ho[uses,] the gambling and other pleasure palaces all provide vivid reminders of the port's early 20th-century heyday.

most stately of streets in
Adelaide, a considerable superlative here, is **North Terrace,**
which delineates the northern
edge of the business district.
North Terrace is lined with trees
and distinguished buildings—
mansions and museums, churches
and memorials.

Between the Terrace and the
gently sloping, landscaped bank

of the river, the **Adelaide**
Festival Centre calls to mind
Sydney's Opera House, but
with angular planes instead of
billowing curves; Adelaide also
truncated Sydney's lavish price
tag. The relatively budget-
priced, 20-million-dollar complex has a theatre for every occasion. The 2,000-seat Festival
Theatre is convertible, in three
hours, from an opera house to

nor[th?]
the Murr[ay?]
Great Austra[lian?]

142

a concert hall with outstanding acoustics. A drama theatre seats some 600 people, an experimental theatre 350. There are hourly backstage tours of the establishment. Outside, bold sculptures are strewn around the plaza. You can eat outdoors in a Festival Centre bistro overlooking the river, or make your own picnic on the lawn. Or take a sightseeing boat up the river to the **Zoo,** where you can pet the kangaroos and admire an outstanding collection of Australian birds.

Behind the Festival Centre, the South Australian **Parliament House** is dignified by ten Corinthian columns and altogether

Adelaide youngsters try out the pleasures of topical sculpture.

so much expensive stonework it was nicknamed the marble palace. The foundation was laid in 1881 but work continued, on and off, over the following 58 years. Next door, the **Constitutional Museum** occupies the former Legislative Council building. It's Australia's only museum of political history.

A startling change of pace lies in ambush just next door: **Adelaide Casino** is the new name of the game in a dazzling conversion of the vastly cupolated old railway station. They've created an uncompromisingly plush

gambling den which, despite the potted palms, marble floors and mighty chandeliers, is open (until 4 a.m.) to ordinary people. Most of the clients seem to favour keno, a bingoesque game, to the complexities of blackjack, roulette, baccarat and other international pastimes on offer.

Elsewhere along North Terrace, the **University of Adelaide** is at the heart of a cluster of cultural institutions. Whale skeletons fill the show windows of the **South Australian Museum** as a come-on. Inside, a monumental collection of Aboriginal

Wilful Wombat

The hairy-nosed wombat (Vom-
...us lasiorhinus latifrons, to give
...' credentials) can survive in
... like a camel—by going
... seemingly as long as
the camel, this soft-
... is quite friendly
... y one,
... which the
...ay gets
about the size of piglets.

too warm. When the weather's cool, the animal may sunbathe at the entrance to its lair. Somewhat headstrong, the wombat prefers to go through, rather than round, obstacles. It is equipped with a unique defence system: a hard bony plate in its rump. Any predator that follows the wombat down its burrow with evil intentions is likely to find itself crushed to death against the ceiling. Like the kangaroo, to which it is distantly related, the wombat gives birth to an unfinished baby, which develops in the mother's pouch.

Perhaps a million years ago a giant ancestor of the wombat family roamed Australia. Phascolonus gigas grew as big as a hippopotamus. But modern wombats are about the size of piglets.

artefacts includes extraordinary sculptures collected in the Lake Eyre region by a turn-of-the-century Lutheran missionary. Among them: a group of bow-legged dogs modelled in resin extracted from the desert's spinifex grass. Other countries are well represented in a comprehensive survey of ceremonial masks, shields and sculptures from South Pacific islands. And you can see a traditional trading vessel from New Guinea, which remained in service until recent times, with a bamboo deck and a sail made of bark. The museum also features a didactic display of stuffed Australian animals, reptiles, birds and fish.

The **Art Gallery of South Australia** covers centuries of the world's art, from ancient Chinese ceramics to contemporary Australian prints, drawings, paintings and sculptures. Some of the modern works are staggeringly avant-garde.

Two more of the historic buildings on North Terrace: **Holy Trinity Church,** the first Anglican church built in South Australia (begun in 1838); and **Ayers House,** a 45-room mansion furnished in opulent 19th-century style. The house was owned by a local businessman and statesman, Sir Henry Ayers, after whom an admiring explorer named Ayers Rock.

Parallel with North Terrace,

Rundle Mall, a destrian mall, Adelaide's shop trademark is a ture comprising spheres of stainle ing the animation all around. The mall's merchants include big department stores, boutiques, cafés and restaurants. Street entertainers are usually on hand to sing, dance, play or mime in hopes of garnering a few coins. Rundle Street's westward extension, **Hindley Street,** is more cosmopolitan and slightly rakish, with restaurants of many nation-

---

Floating in Adelaide

Homesick Spaniards miss paella, expatriate Russians crave borscht, and anyone exiled from Adelaide can do nothing but dream of the renowned pie floater. It's found only in South Australia.

A pie floater is a substantial meat pie marooned bottom up in a sea of thick pea soup. An anticlimax of tomato sauce is sometimes added. This native delicacy may not sound exactly irresistible, but the aroma is, and then the taste. You have to be part of the atmosphere, standing at the counter of a pie wagon, with a cup of coffee to complete the late night snack. The principal hangout of pie floater fans is at Victoria Square, where a well-equipped specialist van is moored.

coffee bars, amusement ...des, and even strip clubs and adult" book stores.

For another kind of shopping experience, have a look at the **Central Market** in Grote Street. This carnival of fresh fruits and vegetables is said to be the biggest produce market in the southern hemisphere.

North of the city centre, **Light's Vision** is not a sound-and-light show, as its name may suggest. It's a monument to the foresight of Lieutenant-Colonel William Light, who was sent out in 1836 to find the ideal site for a model city, then devise the total plan for its development. Atop a pedestal on Montefiore Hill, his statue peers over the parklands, pointing at the city of Adelaide, which he created.

Nearby Places

Adelaide has an outstanding public transport system, including the last word in buses—a "bullet bus" that steers itself along its own smooth roadway. But nostalgia persists: the last surviving tramcars still clatter along between the edge of Victoria Square and the seashore at suburban **Glenelg**. This old-fashioned beach resort, from which a fishing pier forges far out to sea, was the original landing place of the colonists who founded South Australia. A full-size replica of their vessel, a con-

verted freighter named *HMAS Buffalo,* moored nearby, serves as a museum and restaurant.

Among other **beaches** near Adelaide, from north to south along the Gulf of St. Vincent: Semaphore, Grange, Henley Beach, West Beach, Somerton, Brighton and Seacliff.

The **Adelaide Hills,** the last manifestation of the Flinders Ranges, south and east of the city, provide a background of forests, orchards and vineyards. There are pleasant drives, walks, views and picnic possibilities. The highest of the hills, **Mount Lofty** (770 metres [2,500 feet]) is only half an hour out of town by car. You can look down on the hang-gliding enthusiasts riding the hot air currents on the leisurely route back to sea level.

Hahndorf, a hill village about 30 kilometres (less than 20 miles) south-east of Adelaide, has changed little since it was settled in 1839 by German refugees. To the delight of sightseers, many of the original buildings have been restored in this oldest surviving German settlement in Australia. A number of folklore events brighten the tourist calendar, especially a marksmanship and beer-drinking festival every January.

Well-travelled tuba resounds at Barossa folk festival.

148

Up the River

When it comes to the **Murray** ... , the Australians go into ... orts of delight. Having ... rs, they are thrilled ... al equivalent of the ... the Murray begins ... Mountains (the ... becomes the ... ctoria and ... d enjoys ... th the ... The

river accounts for the beautiful vineyards, orchards and pastures along the way, not to mention the boating, fishing and water-skiing. In the 19th century the river was a main highway for passengers and cargo, but the advent of railroads and high-ways left the Murray more of a pleasure route.

Paddle steamers churn up nostalgia along the lower Murray, only an hour's drive from Ade-

great navigator named the place Kangaroo Island. Right behind the Flinders expedition came a French explorer, Nicolas Baudin. Having lost the territorial claim to the British, he contributed some French names to the island's features. They're still on the map: places like D'Estrees Bay, Cape Du Couëdic and Cape D'Estaing. Later settlers acknowledged Baudin's effort and built a white-domed monument at Hog Bay, called **Frenchmans Rock.**

The capital of Kangaroo Island, **Kingscote,** has a permanent population of about 1,200 and an elongated pier. This is where the roll-on/roll-off ferry from

Corrugated iron makes a practical roof for many a charming homestead.

Port Adelaide docks; the island's airfield is only a few kilometres inland. Dolphins and seals frolic just off shore.

In 1919 the western end of the island was designated a nature reserve. **Flinders Chase National Park** is South Australia's biggest. This is not a zoo; the animals are in their natural state, but in the absence of predators the kangaroos, koalas and emus have become extroverts, snuggling up to the visitors and trying to sponge or steal some food.

On the south coast, **Seal Bay** belongs to Australian sea lions. They are so unafraid of humans that you can wander among them at will, except in certain fenced-off areas. Birdwatchers thrill to local species which show clear differences from mainland relatives, and a noisy population of migratory birds from distant oceans.

Why "Kangaroo?"

The story goes that Captain James Cook, the 18th-century explorer, asked an Aborigine to tell him the name of the strange hopalong marsupial. "Kangaroo," said his informant. Captain Cook duly informed the world. Much later, it turned out that "kangaroo" is a native expression for "I don't know."

Kangaroos come in all sizes, from the red—often taller than a man—to the musk kangaroo, no taller than a year-old child. With their deer-like faces and congenial personalities, kangaroos can be very appealing. But not to farmers whose grain they appropriate.

The joey, born in an embryonic stage, moves into the mother's pouch for about six months of nursing. Kangaroos can limit the chain of reproduction in time of drought or disaster, putting an embryo in limbo until conditions improve. Thus the race prospers ... by leaps and bounds.

154

THREE PENINSULAS

Just south of Adelaide, the **Fleurieu Peninsula** is an easy-to-reach, easy-to-like holidayland of surfing beaches, vineyards and history. The history starts at the beginning of the 19th century when the French explorer Baudin named the peninsula after his Navy minister, Count Pierre de Fleurieu. The first industry on the peninsula was whaling, based at **Victor Harbour.** It's now the biggest town, and a very popular year-round resort.

Another historic place is **Maslin's Beach,** on the Gulf St. Vincent coast. Here a new leaf was turned in the evolution of Australian social customs. This was the nation's first legal nudists' beach.

Inland, the peninsula's fame comes from scores of vineyards basking in the sunshine of the **Southern Vales.** They've been making wine here since 1838, to great effect. Many of the wineries encourage connoisseurs or simply wine-drinkers to stop in and try the vintages, though you needn't feel guilty if you taste and run. The best-known area of wine production is **McLaren Vale.**

The **Yorke Peninsula,** west of Adelaide, first became important in the 19th century as a copper mining district. Most of the miners were imported from Cornwall, England's copper-rich

south-western peninsula, and the Cornish touch can still be seen in the design of the old cottages and churches. Museums and the ruins of the copper mine superstructures provide constant reminders of the area's heyday, which lasted until the 1920s. They've even kept up the homely tradition of baking Cornish pasties.

The **Eyre Peninsula** encompasses beach resorts, wheat fields, bushland, industrial centres and a prized wilderness, **Lincoln National Park.** Atop magnificent cliffs at the tip of the peninsula, the park is home to kangaroos and birds as diverse as emus, parrots and sea eagles. Fishing boats big and small are anchored in the attractive deepwater harbour of **Port Lincoln**, the tuna-fishing capital of Australia. The biggest city on the peninsula, **Whyalla**, grew on a solid base of heavy industry—as heavy as iron and steel. If a blast furnace is your cup of tea, you can join one of the daily tours of the local steelworks; the public can also visit the iron-mining area.

The Eyre Peninsula reaches as far west as **Ceduna,** where the endless expanse of the **Nullarbor Plain** begins. It's more than 1,200 kilometres (some 750 miles) from Ceduna westward to the next town of any significance (Norseman, W.A.). Filling sta-

No fear of falling asleep, with these deadly perils on the prowl.

tions do occur, but the route is lonely and gruelling. Nullarbor is Latin for "treeless", an indication that the plain is also waterless. But, as the Aborigines were always aware, water is there if you know where to look: underground in limestone caverns. The highway follows the dunes and cliffs along the **Great Australian Bight,** which forms the bulk of the continent's curving southern coast.

FLINDERS RANGES

For scenic splendour, South Australia's Outback competes well with the remote areas of the other states, nowhere more impressively than in the Flinders Ranges. Rising from a landscape

156

saucer is about 20 kilometres (12 miles) long and 8 kilometres (5 miles) wide. Wilpena Pound is not only spectacular as a scenic and geological curiosity; it wins admiring squawks from the bird-watchers. Here you can spot butcherbirds, wagtails, galahs, honeyeaters and wedge-tailed eagles.

An Explorer's Endurance

Imagine the feat of the British explorer John Eyre, who took more than a year to make the first overland trek from Adelaide to the south-west corner of Western Australia. Arriving at Albany, W.A., in July, 1841, he accepted congratulations, a glass of hot brandy, a bath, and a fresh suit of clothes. The least a later generation could do was name Route 1 the Eyre Highway.

John Eyre is also celebrated in the names of the Eyre Peninsula, which he explored, and Lake Eyre, Australia's largest salt lake, which he discovered. In the desert some 640 kilometres (400 miles) north of Adelaide, Lake Eyre is normally so dry its salty crust has been used as the track for world speed records. When the rare rains do come, however, the scene changes drastically: the lake floods, birds convene and flowers bloom along the lakeshore. But the lake has only filled twice in the memory of white man.

---

as flat as the sea, the tinted peaks speak poetry to lovers of robust scenery. In the spring the rugged wooded hillsides come to life with a flood of wild flowers, but at any time of year the scene is intriguing. The mountains, like the desert, are much more colourful at close range.

The top phenomenon of the Flinders Ranges is a huge natural basin called **Wilpena Pound.** Rimmed by sheer cliffs, the

157

The flat floor of the Pound is perfectly designed for bush walks (suggested routes are sign-posted). But not in summer, when it's altogether too hot for unnecessary exertions. In any season it's essential to carry a supply of drinking water. There's only one way into the amphitheatre, through a narrow gorge occupied in rainy times by the Wilpena Creek.

An area of such grandeur was bound to inspire Aboriginal myths and art over thousands of years. Timeless rock paintings can be inspected near Wilpena at Arkaroo and at Yourambulla, south of the village of Hawker.

Collectors' Rocks

An opal is simply hydrous silica, a jumble of submicroscopic crystals with little to commend it except its beauty. Diamonds, after all, are not only a girl's best friend but can be used for industrial purposes. But opals are good for nothing except jewellery.

Opals come in many colours: white, yellow, green, blue, red or black. The highly prized black opals come from Lightning Ridge, New South Wales. Coober Pedy is best known for its white or milky opals. In 1956 an opal weighing 7½ pounds was unearthed at Coober Pedy. The price was $1.7 million. You might want to buy a less ostentatious one.

COOBER PEDY

The town the opals come from must rate as one of the most bizarre tourist attractions anywhere. When you say "desert" this is what it means: in the summer the daytime temperature can reach 45 °C (113 °F) to 50 °C (122 °F). That's in the shade, of which supplies are extremely limited. In winter the nights become unpleasantly cold. Yet a couple of thousand people make their home in this far corner of the Outback.

The name Coober Pedy comes from an Aboriginal phrase meaning "white fellow's hole in the ground". And indeed the settlers have survived here by

burrowing hobbit-like into the side of a low hill. Thus insulated, the temperatures within are constant and comfortable, regardless of the excesses outside. Among the dugouts are residences of some luxury, complete with electricity and wall-to-wall carpets. Also underground are a Roman Catholic chapel, a bank and an air-conditioned motel.

Regular tours by bus or plane bring the curious crowds to Coober Pedy, about 950 kilometres (nearly 600 miles) northwest of Adelaide. The tours visit the local opal fields, where most of the world's opals are produced, with demonstrations of opal cutting and polishing.

Pages 158–159: Flamboyant Simpson Desert. Above: Gigantic insects fossick among the mullock heaps in Coober Pedy.

Having learned the intricacies, you can buy finished stones and jewellery on the spot. Or try noodling in the mullock heaps: all you need is a rake or a sieve to sift through the rubble at the top of each mineshaft, and if you're lucky you may find an overlooked opal. Amateur fortune-seekers need a permit (obtainable from the Mines Department in Adelaide) to go fossicking.

161

VICTORIA

By Australian standards, the state of Victoria is a midget. About the same size as Great Britain, and barely bigger than, say, Minnesota, it is the smallest state on the mainland. But nearly 4 million inhabitants give Victoria the nation's highest population density.

Seven out of ten Victorians live in the capital, Melbourne, a hub of finance, industry, culture and sports. The sophisticated city folk live within easy striking distance of the state's bushland and 19th-century boomtowns, the sea, the vineyards and ski slopes. Some of the scenery is so rich and pretty that the state's first name was *Australia Felix* —Latin for bountiful or lucky.

Victoria was the earliest state to industrialize, and today manufacturing accounts for the bulk of the economy. But it's still a leading farming power, hence the nickname, "Garden State". The agricultural potential was al-

most unexploited until the 1860s, after the state's gold rush fizzled. Unemployed ex-prospectors eagerly fanned out as farmers, working land they could buy for one pound per acre. Immigrants in search of a figurative pot of gold followed in a steady flow that reached a tidal wave after World War II, with the policy of "populate or perish". This produced curious ethnic pockets around the state and the cosmopolitan effervescence of a multicultural society within the dignified confines of the capital city.

MELBOURNE

Elegant parks and gardens splash green patterns across Melbourne's map, softening the rigours of its precise grid plan, and offering merciful breathing space on the edges of the city centre's hubbub. This is a city of *serious* buildings—banks where you know your money is safe, and offices where bureaucrats are worthily enshrined. This air of distinction may have something to do with the fact that the city was founded not by prisoners (as was Sydney) but by ad-

The Yarra River affords Melbourne's most restful perspective.

162

venturous free enterprisers with a vision of success.

It's all so grand you might forget Melbourne's rough-and-tumble pioneering days. The gold rush broke out in Victoria in 1851, only a few months after the fever hit New South Wales. A gold strike at Ballarat so electrified the state that Melbourne itself risked becoming a ghost town; businessmen locked their offices or shops and rushed to the goldfields, and ships were abandoned by their gold-crazed crews. New immigrants, rushing in to fill the gap, lived in shacks and tents. Successful diggers returned to Melbourne with so much money to dispose of that morals loosened lustily.

The long-running rivalry between Sydney and Melbourne is incurable. Sydney thinks Melbourne is boring, Melbourne thinks Sydney is superficial. Sydney blasts Melbourne's climate, Melbourne ridicules Sydney's self-satisfaction. Generally, Melbourne (with less than 3 million inhabitants) seems on the defensive, for instance on the subject of the unpredictable weather; temperatures are subject to extremes. As for Sydney's Opera House, Melbourne was determined to outdo it, but in a "warm and welcoming" way, avoiding what was pointedly called "self-conscious grandeur". The result was the Victorian Arts Centre, a promising security blanket for local self-confidence.

If Melbourne is staid, as Sydneysiders allege, you'd never know it from the tramcars. Art-

Rare reminders of the colourful past, in Melbourne's central district.

ists and cartoonists have been commissioned to paint the sides of the trams, creating an eclectic, electric gallery in motion. Another aspect of the Melbourne character that's anything but stuffy: the sports mania. "Footy"—high-scoring Australian Rules Football—rules here. Cricket is a passion. And as for the horses, the Melbourne Cup is so all-engrossing that the first Tuesday in November, when the race is run, counts as a legal holiday.

Unlike Sydney, Melbourne is a city that empties after dark. Local planners ruled that housing had to be low-rise, so the suburbs sprawl for mile after middleclass mile of houses instead of apartments. Melbourne's nightlife is widely dispersed, but it does exist, from opera and bal-

let to dancing and floorshows. Melbournians also have a reputation as gourmets; before deciding which of 1,300 restaurants to patronize they diligently compare the ratings in the local epicure guidebooks.

City Sights

One pleasant angle on Melbourne is from the level of the **Yarra,** the river embellishing the centre of the city. On the last few miles of its journey to the sea, the Yarra plays host to freighters, pleasure boats and rowing regattas. And it waters the gardens, reflects the skyscrapers, and invites cyclists and joggers to follow its course along prettily landscaped paths. For a look up at the skyline and a close-up of river commerce, take one of the cruise boats that leave from Princes Walk, by Princes Bridge.

Aerial views over the river and the city point up the ample acres of green (contrasting with yellow and russet leaves in autumn) in the parks and gardens scattered among the businesslike blocks. Vantage points include the top of the Regent Hotel, the CML Building or the ICI Building—Australia's first skyscraper in 1958.

An inescapable sight along the waterfront is the **World Trade Centre,** a huge 1980s building meant to house international trade exhibitions. On the opposite bank, the **Polly Woodside,** a square-rigged sailing barque, recalls the adventurous days of the last century. Launched in Ireland in 1885, the restored ship now serves as part of a maritime museum.

Near the river, just south of the very heart of town, an Eiffel-tower-style superstructure marks the modern **Victorian Arts Centre.** This airy silver, gold and white spire rises from flowing curves suggesting a ballet dancer's tutu.

The first part of the complex to open, in 1968, was the **National Gallery of Victoria,** now a high-priority stop for art lovers from all the world. The big collection covers European and Asian art, old and new, and of course a comprehensive look at Australian painting and sculpture. Among the choicest items on show: a vast, anecdotal Tiepolo painting from the 1740s, *The Banquet of Cleopatra;* sculptures by Rodin, Henry Moore and Barbara Hepworth; a first-class survey of classical Chinese porcelain; and a splendid sampling of Australian Aboriginal paintings. The Gallery, founded in 1861, is the oldest such institution in the country. In comfortable modern surroundings it hits its stride with the wealth of Australian paintings from 18th-century discoveries to living masters. And tilt your head back to admire the immense, 10,000-piece stained-glass ceiling of the Great Hall.

The **Theatres Building**, directly beneath the symbolic spire identifying the Arts Centre, is the place to see opera, ballet and modern musicals. Under the same roof are a playhouse for drama and a smaller studio theatre for experimental works. The adjoining **Concert Hall**, which seats 2,700 people, is used for symphony concerts, but the acoustics can be changed to suit other types of performance. If you're not going to a concert, nip in for a glance at the art work in the lobby, or take a guided back-

National Gallery of Victoria—a wide range of exhibits in a fine modern building.

stage tour. The complex caters well to hungry patrons of the arts, with everything from snack bars to luxury-class restaurants.

Just across Princes Bridge on the north side of the river, the spires of **St. Paul's Cathedral** are not as old as they look. They were added in the 1920s, several decades after the original Gothic-style structure was completed. The church is a refreshing hideaway in the midst of the busiest part of the business district, a few steps away from the Victorian mass of the main railway station and a less obvious historic landmark, **Young & Jackson's** pub. In the bar hangs a notorious oil painting of the nude "Chloe"—which has delighted generations of beer drinkers since it scandalized Melbourne's art exhibition of 1880.

City Square, just north of the cathedral, has modern fountains, waterfalls, flowerbeds and outdoor cafés but, according to its critics, not enough character to win the hearts of Melbournians. Built in the 1860s, the **Town Hall,** on the opposite side of Collins Street, is used for concerts and official happenings. It can hold 3,000 people.

Collins Street and the parallel **Bourke Street** are the reason Melbournians claim to have the best shopping in Australia. There are big department stores, small trendy shops, and a warren of arcades for making the most of those rainy hours. The outstanding example of an old-time Melbourne shopping institution, the glass-roofed **Block Arcade,** is an 1892 copy of a Milan landmark, the airy Vittorio Emmanuele Galleria. The Bourke Street **Mall** is a pleasure to roam. Diversions are provided by clowns, magicians, bagpipers and other hopeful talents. But don't get carried away by the relaxed atmosphere: although this is a

---

Almost Batmania

If Australia's governor hadn't tried to butter up his boss, the British prime minister of the day, Melbourne might have been given a silly or undignified name. Among those suggested were Yarra Yarra and, no joking, Batmania, after John Batman—the farsighted operator from Tasmania who bought 100,000 acres from the Aborigines to found the colony. Even if Batman drove a mercilessly hard bargain, buying at all—rather than stealing—was a rare method of acquiring land from the traditional owners.

For reasons of their own the early settlers called the place Bearbrass, a name only an early settler could love. But in 1837 the town was officially named in honour of the head of the government in London, Lord Melbourne, a crony of Queen Victoria herself.

---

pedestrians-only zone, there is one big exception: the trams rattle right down the middle of the mall.

By way of historic buildings, Melbourne likes to show off **Parliament House,** in its own park facing Spring Street. It's been called the finest legislative headquarters this side of London; in fact, many of the furnishings are copies of those in Britain's Palace of Westminster. The federal government used this as its temporary headquarters in Australia's early days. The building, dating from 1854, is open for guided tours when the state parliament is off duty.

Older than any of the well-preserved Victorian buildings is **Captain Cook's Cottage** in Fitzroy Gardens. The great discoverer never lived in Melbourne; the stone house was transplanted in 1934 from Great Ayton in Cook's native Yorkshire. Truthfully, it would be more accurate to call it Cook's *parents' cottage:* there's no evidence that the good captain did live under its tile roof in his 18th-century childhood. The only genuine Cook relic in the place is a small sea chest with the initials J.C.

Only in Australia, it seems, are jails such popular tourist attractions. The most fascinating of all is the **Old Melbourne Gaol,** just across the street from the modern Police Headquarters on Russell Street. Opened in 1854, the three-storey penitentiary was the scene of more than 100 hangings. Death masks of the most famous prisoners are displayed, along with other penal memorabilia, such as a "lashing triangle", last used in the enlightened year of 1958. The best known character on death row, Ned Kelly, the celebrated bushranger, was executed here on Melbourne Cup Day 1880. The jail displays the weird suit of improvised armour he was wearing when captured.

Melbourne's Trams

Tramcars are as much a part of Melbourne's character as Victorian architecture and football madness. The new trams are sleek and comfortable, the old ones worthy as relics. Quite a few have been decorated by talented local artists to constitute a travelling mural.

Keep well clear of these 70-ton trams. To accommodate them, Melbourne traffic is organized in a somewhat eccentric way. If you're driving, you can pass a stationary tram—at a maximum of 10 kilometres per hour—only if a policeman or uniformed tramway employee gives the go-ahead. Trams have the right of way at crossroads; at certain main intersections, if you want to turn right, you have to move to the left lane, after the trams have passed, then wait for the light to change before turning right.

VICTORIA

The most luscious fruit, the plumpest of vegetables, displayed with care in Queen Victoria Market.

And you can step inside the executive-sized cell that was his last residence on earth; it has a fine view of the gallows.

The **National Museum** looks not too promising if you enter through the Russell Street entrance, just down the street from the jail. Old-fashioned zoological exhibits are stuffed under glass. But it gets better and brighter as you proceed through rooms and labyrinthine corridors. Among the principal subjects are natural history, geology and anthropology, and there are imaginatively equipped rooms where children can get to grips with the exhibits. The museum's most visited display is an equine shrine: the taxidermist's version of Phar Lap, a chestnut gelding considered the greatest racehorse in the nation's history, and still a national hero. He won the 1930 Melbourne Cup by three lengths. Phar Lap's heart suddenly failed in 1932, after he won California's Agua Caliente Handicap.

Now for something livelier. Melbourne's **Chinatown** centres on Little Bourke Street, east of Swanston Street. Special street lights and gates define the area, where Chinese restaurants are jammed shoulder to shoulder with cafés, a church, small factories and exotic shops. The area has had a unique flavour since the gold-rush days, when fortune-hunters from China crowded into this low-rent district before and after their efforts in the bush. Chinatown today glows on the maps of local gourmets.

So does **Queen Victoria Market,** which sums up the bounty

of Australian agriculture. Just about everything that grows is here, piled up in irresistibly fresh pyramids. It's as if the best fruit and vegetables had been creamed from every market from Sweden to Sicily. The best time to take in the atmosphere is early in the morning; Queen Victoria Market is closed Mondays and Wednesdays. On Sundays it becomes a flea market for cheap clothing and bric-a-brac.

Parks and Gardens

South of the river, the **Royal Botanic Gardens** are classed among the finest in the world. Thirty-six hectares (nearly 90 acres) of superb rolling landscape remind the visitor that Melbourne enjoys four seasons. Each time of year has its specialities, and seasonal leaflets are issued for guide-yourself walks. For Australians, some of the joy of this park is the selection of

171

brightly tinted trees and plants from the northern hemisphere. A total of 13,000 species are represented here, beside the lovely lawns and lakes.

Between the Botanic Gardens and **Kings Domain** stands the imposing **Government House**, the state governor's mansion, and **La Trobe's Cottage,** its early 19th-century predecessor. The timber cottage was shipped out from Britain as a prefabricated home for Charles La Trobe, who became Victoria's first Lieutenant-Governor in 1851. One of La Trobe's achievements was to establish a wine industry in Victoria. Across from the cottage, the massive **Shrine of Remembrance** commemorates the Australians who fell in World War I; tragically, more than 60 per cent of all Australian troops were either killed or wounded in the "war to end all wars". Once a year, every Armistice Day, at 11 a.m., a beam of sunlight coming through an opening in the roof strikes the Rock of Remembrance.

In Parkville, north of the city centre, the **Royal Melbourne Zoo** charms foreigners with kangaroos, koalas, platypuses and the like, while amazing the locals with an all-star cast of elephants, giraffes, monkeys and other animals from afar. And there's a walk-through aviary. The zoo is open 365 days a year.

Suburbs

The inner city suburb of **Carlton** combines the restored elegance of Victorian architecture with contemporary dynamism. The latter may be attributed to the area's large immigrant colony, mostly Italian. Hence the profusion of outdoor cafés, pizzerias, trattorias and gelaterias.

In **South Yarra**, about 2 hectares (5 acres) of lawns and gardens surround Melbourne's finest stately home, **Como House.** Now run by the National Trust, this example of the colonial era's high style was completed with the addition of a gold and white ballroom in the 1870s. For a breath of air, each of its two storeys was built with wide verandahs decorated with intricate ironwork.

Toorak, the snootiest of suburbs, is said to harbour more money than any other suburb in Australia. The mansions, nicely landscaped, make tourists and most other passers-by stand and gape. Shopping on the Toorak Road is full of stylish delights.

A totally different shopping experience awaits in the seaside suburb of **St. Kilda.** On Sundays its Esplanade is taken over by artists, antique dealers and flea market entrepreneurs of every sort. Ackland Street's restaurants, cafés and bakeries preserve a middle-European Jewish flavour.

EXCURSIONS

A favourite day trip from Melbourne is to the **Dandenong Ranges,** volcanic mountains where flowered hillsides and eucalyptus forests set the scene for total relaxation. Only an hour's drive from town, the hills won't take your breath away. Mount Dandenong itself claims an altitude of only 633 metres (2,077 feet).

One highlight of a day among the small towns, farms, parks and gardens of the Dandenongs is a ride on **Puffing Billy,** a restored old steam train plying 13 kilometres (8 miles) of narrow-gauge track. The line was seriously devoted to passenger operations from 1900 to 1958. Four years later it was converted to the tourism business. The train never achieves great speed. In fact, an annual race pits Puffing Billy against hundreds of runners.

The **William Ricketts Sanctuary** is an extraordinary collection of sculpture by a loner who was obsessed with Aboriginal culture and its near-destruction by his fellow whites. Ricketts carved the most lifelike faces of Aborigines, accompanied by their spiritual symbols. The result is unorthodox, even unnerving.

Not for Cuddling

The echidna or spiny anteater, native to Australia and New Guinea, might be nice to know if it weren't so hard to get close to. Covered in hedgehog-style spines, and unapproachable at the best of times, this shy animal rolls itself into a prickly ball to repel any danger.

About the size of a tomcat, the echidna is best known to ants and termites as the fellow with the prodigious tongue that flicks out to zap its prey. Also formidable are its oversized claws, which can excavate termite nests or dig a quick escape hatch.

The echidna is a monotreme—an egg-laying mammal like the platypus. The egg matures in a kangaroo-like pouch. When the baby anteater grows too bristly for comfort, the mother prudently builds it a nest in the ground.

In **Sherbrooke Forest Park** you can give your lungs a treat, savouring the elixir of ferns and mountain ash and whatever flowers happen to be abloom. The forest is immensely tall, with mountain ash monuments as high as 20-storey buildings and ferns as big as palm trees. This is the place to see, or at least hear, the lyrebird, a great mimic; it does imitations of other birds, human voices and even inanimate objects like passing cars. Among the animal residents of the park is the echidna, alias the spiny anteater.

Healesville, less than 60 kilometres (40 miles) east of Melbourne, is the place to go for an intimate look at Australian animals on their home ground. The **Fauna Sanctuary,** nearby in the Yarra Valley, contains more than 200 native species, such as kangaroos, wombats and emus. The animals feel quite comfortable with humans about, and many come up to mingle with the visitors, hoping to share a picnic. The sanctuary was founded in 1921 as a research establishment for the study of the local fauna.

The Yarra Valley was the site of the first commercial winery in the state, dating back to the middle of the 19th century. After drastic ups and downs, the region's vineyards are again doing well, and are worth a wine-tasting outing.

Penguin Parade

For a magical experience for adults and children, try a long day trip to **Phillip Island,** home of the fairy penguins. These mini-

Listen for the lyrebird in Sherbrooke Forest—only a few hops away from the city.

penguins have always used the island as their base. Hundreds of them come home at sunset; the number varies depending on activities at sea, where they spend most of their time fishing. For reasons of their own, perhaps sensing danger, they tread water off shore until night falls before venturing onto the beach. After decades of being stared at by visitors they still feel insecure arriving on the island.

Before dusk, hundreds of tourists gather behind ropes on Summerland Beach and in viewing stands on the sandhills above. As the spotlights go on, announcements in English and Japanese warn the visitors not to touch or upset the penguins: no flash cameras, no running, no violent movements. The penguins observe all this and wait for the first star to appear in the sky.

The first brave penguin scout scrambles onto dry land and, suspiciously, lurches across the beach and up the hill to his burrow. In small groups the others follow. It can take half an hour or more for all the birds that are coming ashore to arrive.

Waddling Mini-Penguins

The fairy penguin, smallest of all penguins, is an Australian exclusive. It struts across the beach with a concentrated but unsuccessful effort to look sober. But the bird is out of its element; it swims better than it walks. In the cold southern sea, its body insulated by waterproof feathers, the penguin swims effortlessly many miles from home—as far as is necessary to find the squid, pilchard and anchovy it likes to eat.

At sunset the fairy penguin, no bigger than a seagull, comes back to its nest in the dune to feed the chicks. The young stay in the burrow for a couple of months before learning how to swim. When the flock return from the sea, long

conversations, perhaps even quarrels, go on into the night, within families and from burrow to burrow.

Phillip Island, which is 120 kilometres (75 miles) south-east of Melbourne, receives about 2 million visitors a year. It's linked to the mainland by a bridge at San Remo. The penguins are the stars, but the supporting cast is also worth seeing: thousands of fur seals residing on tall rocks on the west coast; clouds of mutton birds arriving every November; and a colony of koalas, vegetating in the high branches of the gum trees. Take a sweater or coat for the penguin parade, for the night breeze here is very chill even in summer.

Wilsons Promontory

Until the Ice Age, the southernmost tip of the Australian mainland was connected to Tasmania. When the ice melted the heights became an island. Since then the dunes built up, linking the massive promontory to the rest of Victoria. The scenery is varied and spectacular, making Wilsons Promontory the state's most popular national park.

The coastline ranges from magnificent granite headlands to peaceful sandy beaches. Walking tracks go through forests and moorland and flower-covered heathland. Koalas live here, as do kangaroos and emus. Known locally as "The Prom", the peninsula is about 240 kilometres (150 miles) south-east of Melbourne.

THE GOLDFIELDS

A drive of 113 kilometres (70 miles) west of Melbourne takes you well over a century back in time to the attractive town of **Ballarat**, rich with all the atmosphere of Australia's golden age. This is gold-rush country, and it's still a prize destination for tourists.

Ballarat has a bitter-sweet history. Gold was discovered in 1851, and thousands of miners trekked to the fields. The early arrivals simply scooped up a fortune, but latecomers had to work harder, following the ore ever deeper.

Almost from the outset the government collected a licence fee from the miners. Many newcomers couldn't afford to pay a tax on hope, so they tended to lie low when the licence inspectors swooped. In the midst of growing antagonism between the authorities and the miners, charges of murder and official corruption pushed the diggers to revolt. In the Eureka Rebellion, Australia's first and only uprising, insurgent miners were besieged in their stockade. An uneven battle cost many lives, mostly diggers. The nation was stunned. The anguish endured for years, inspiring poets and politicians.

When peace returned to the goldfields, and many of the miners' grievances were answered, Ballarat went back to the business of making a fortune. In 1858 a group of Cornishmen came upon what they called the Welcome Nugget: 63,000 grams. It was eventually put on show in the Crystal Palace in London before being minted. Parallel with the discovery of wealth, Ballarat grew into a stately town where even art and good taste had their day.

To see what Ballarat was like in the 1850s, visit **Sovereign Hill,** an open-air museum re-creating the sights, sounds and smells of the gold rush. Local folk, dressed in Victorian-era clothing, operate the shops, post office, bakery and printing office of what appears to be a real town. Tourists are invited to try their hand with a digger's pan, under expert instruction. The **Gold Museum** traces the history of the mineral since biblical times and displays notable nuggets and gold coins.

In the real Ballarat, the principal public buildings on the wide tree-lined streets are a long-lasting monument to the good old days. Some of those who got rich quick had the good taste to spend some of their money on the finer things. Hence the statues of mythological subjects in Carrara marble in the **Botanical Gardens,** and the admirable collection of early Australian art in the **Ballarat Fine Art Gallery.**

Another treat for nostalgia fans is the town of **Bendigo,** 150 kilometres (93 miles) north-west of Melbourne. The name is a very roundabout corruption of Abednego, the Old Testament companion of Shadrach and Meshach. In the 1850s, Bendigo Creek, running through the centre of town, was awash with panning miners.

The **Central Deborah Mine** is now a museum of 19th-century mining technology. From there you can take a "Talking" Tram, an antique vehicle rigged up for tourists on an 8-kilometre (5-mile) historic itinerary. The last stop is the **joss house.** One curiosity of Bendigo was the size of the Chinese population. Chinese miners, who enjoyed less than harmony with their white neighbours, worshipped in a prayer house constructed of timber and hand-made bricks. It's filled with relics of the early Chinese fortune-hunters.

Among the impressive Victorian-era buildings in Bendigo is the **Shamrock Hotel,** lavishly restored to its old grandeur. Dame Nellie Melba, the fabled opera singer, once stayed there. Her real name was Helen Porter Mitchell. Born near Melbourne in 1861, she adapted the city's name for her stage name. Admirers were inspired to perpetuate her fame with creations like melba toast and peach melba.

TASMANIA

If you thought of Tasmania as the last stop before the South Pole, you're right; the Antarctic expeditions actually take off from Hobart. No matter what direction you're heading, though, it's a staging post you hate to leave. Tasmania's scenery owes more to solar than polar influences. Although snow covers the hills in winter, it's a verdant island enjoying a temperate climate. Summer even brings shirtsleeve weather, and you can find palm trees as well as poplars and oaks for some shade.

Suspended 240 kilometres (150 miles) south of southernmost mainland Australia, Tasmania is small only by the swollen standards of the continent. With an area of about 68,000 square kilometres (more than 26,000 square miles), it's bigger than Sri Lanka or Switzerland.

Tassie, as the state is familiarly known, calls itself the Holiday Isle and pushes tourism. Its early residents would have had a bitter laugh at that, interspersed with an oath or two, for the island used to be the place the really incorrigible prisoners were sent. If humble embezzlers and petty larcenists were transported to Sydney, the mass murderers and escape artists tended to be tagged for Tasmania.

Early explorers happened upon Tasmania because it lies on the 40th parallel—the Roaring Forties, along which an unfailing westerly wind blows around the globe. Their sailing ships could hardly miss the place. But that's not to diminish the achievement of the Dutch navigator, Abel Tasman, who gets credit for discovering the island in 1642. He named it after his sponsor, Anton Van Diemen, the governor of the Dutch East Indies. The Dutch never saw a future for the island, and Britain eventually claimed it only to cut out the French. Because of the cruel conditions inflicted on the British prisoners, Van Diemen's Land acquired a sinister reputation. The very name could send a shiver down a sinner's spine. The transportation of convicts was abolished in 1852, and three years later the name was changed to Tasmania in memory of its discoverer and to improve the image.

Since then it's been one triumph after another, as successive waves of free settlers developed an enviably amiable, relaxed way of life. If you like wild scenery, uncrowded historic towns, and open-hearted people, you could easily become a Tasmaniac.

Constitution Dock: a happy coexistence of business and pleasure.

HOBART

Everybody knows that Sydney Harbour is the exciting one, glamorous and instantly recognizable all over the world. Hobart is the lovable harbour, a perfect ocean port on a dreamy river, with soft mountains rising beyond. It might have been transplanted from quite another seafaring latitude, as brisk and tidy as, say, Bergen or Helsinki.

You never know what kind of ships you'll see here: freighters from Singapore, floating fish factories from Japan, or yachts from distant islands, perhaps Britain or Bermuda. The arrival of an ancient sealer, whaler or windjammer would be right in character. Sails still matter here: Hobart's Constitution Dock is the goal line of the gruelling Sydney-to-Hobart yacht race.

Wiping Out the Aborigines

When Van Diemen's Land was first settled, the island's Aborigines may have numbered between 3,000 and 7,000. They were different from the mainland Aborigines, in looks and culture; the native Tasmanians had nothing so advanced as a boomerang.

As the British seized the land and wiped out the animals and birds the indigenous tribes needed for food, the Aborigines fought back with primitive punitive attacks. Enraged, the white men retaliated with their stupendous technological advantage. The survivors of this pogrom were exiled to Flinders Island, an inauspicious outpost best known for its shipwrecks. In spite of belated efforts to protect the race, the last of the fullblooded Tasmanian tribesmen died in 1876.

Aboriginal artefacts are on show at the Tasmanian Museum on Argyle Street in Hobart.

Hobart, Australia's second oldest capital city, has kept a powerful array of historic monuments, from stately official buildings to quaint cottages. Best of all, they're spick and span and still in use.

Another, more recent historical distinction: Hobart was chosen as the site of Australia's first legal casino. The Wrest Point complex grew into an all-round recreation centre, topped by the almost inevitable provincial status symbol, a revolving rooftop restaurant.

With a population approaching 175,000 (suburbs included), Hobart is small enough to get around and get to know, and as unsophisticated and satisfying as the local fish and chips.

City Sights

In this deepwater port, the ships come right into the centre of town. The waterfront, always colourful, is the place to start seeing the city on foot. You can watch crates of giant crabs and scallops come ashore, and follow their destiny to the floating fast-food restaurants moored here. Just behind **Constitution Dock,** where the yacht races end, the late Victorian-era **Customs House** stands out as one of the city's most imposing sandstone monuments. It was built at the turn of the century on the site of one of the colony's oldest landmarks, the original customs house.

Also bordering the docks, **Salamanca Place** is a long row of sandstone warehouses from the 1830s, restored and proudly occupied by artisans' workshops, boutiques and restaurants. On Saturday mornings, stalls selling arts and crafts, knick-knacks, flowers and vegetables cover the cobblestones; jugglers, mimes and minstrels perform and pass the hat.

Altogether more serious is **Parliament House,** also facing the waterfront, from 1840. The state's bicameral legislature operates in a low-rise stone building enjoying some admirable architectural details.

Another venerable structure still in use is the **Theatre Royal** on Campbell Street, Australia's oldest live theatre. Built in the most exquisitely luxurious style in 1834, it has featured stars like Noel Coward and Laurence Olivier.

Overlooking Salamanca Place, **Battery Point** is the historic heart of Hobart, beautifully preserved. The battery in question was a set of coastal artillery guns installed in 1818. Ten years later signal flags were added, for relaying the big news of the day, such as ship arrivals or prison breaks. The area is worth an hour or two of exploration afoot, to absorb the atmosphere

of the narrow streets, the mansions and cottages, churches and taverns. One of the upper-class colonial homes has been turned into the **Van Diemen's Land Memorial Folk Museum,** devoted to the colony's 19th-century way of life, from toys to farm equipment.

The oldest military establishment still in use in Australia, **Anglesea Barracks,** was built by

convicts on a hill site chosen by Governor Lachlan Macquarie in 1811. The design and workmanship of the old buildings can be admired from outside, but to enter the original Officers' Mess or the Military Jail, for example, you have to make arrangements in advance.

The centre of Hobart is linked to the suburbs and the airport by the graceful **Tasman Bridge** across the **Derwent River.** The prestressed concrete bridge ran into trouble in 1975; more accurately, trouble ran into the bridge. A bulk ore carrier, off course, ploughed into the span; tragically, four cars tumbled into the river and the ship sank.

Tasmania—once a dreaded name, now a peaceful holiday haven.

At **Wrest Point,** the nation's first legal **casino** combines gambling, eating, drinking, dancing and floor shows in a one-stop entertainment centre. The big prize is the view from the top of the circular mini-skyscraper encompassing the associated hotel.

For an even more expansive panorama of Hobart and the valley of the Derwent, ascend **Mount Wellington,** the city's eternal landmark. It is named in appreciation of the Duke of Wellington, who toppled Napoleon at Waterloo. For this expedition you can forget your mountain-climbing equipment. A paved road goes all the way to Mount Wellington's summit, 1,270 metres (4,167 feet) above the sea. Snow is a frequent visitor to the mountain during the winter—an exciting novelty for tourists from more northerly Australian climes—but it rarely blocks the road.

Excursions from Hobart

An industrial establishment may not sound like much of an idea for an excursion, but a popular destination up the river at Claremont is a **chocolate factory** belonging to the Cadbury-Schweppes group. The chocolate's local ingredient is

Tame Little Devil

With its big pink ears, mousy face and flamboyant whiskers, this little devil may not win your heart at first sight. Don't let its ferocious looks or its name (origin unknown) put you off. The Tasmanian Devil (Sarcophilus harrisi) is mild of manner and clean. It even washes its face.

The Tasmanian Devil, the size of a small dog, is the largest meat-eating marsupial. Meat is only one of the items in its variable diet, which extends to fish and shellfish, birds and carrion. Flexibility is one reason it has survived; another is that its only enemies are dingoes and foxes, neither of which lives on the island. Devils are still quite common in the Tasmanian countryside, though not very visible because they travel by night.

milk; all the rest is imported from the mainland or beyond. Guided tours of the assembly line attract sweet-toothed visitors of all ages, but tots under eight have to be carried. Visitors can look forward to some samples from the 20,000 tons of annual production.

At **Taroona,** beyond Wrest Point, you can visit the remains, more than a century old, of a different kind of factory, the **Shot Tower.** Though it looks like an ordinary smokestack, this tower 60 metres (nearly 200 feet) tall was used in the manufacture of gunshot and musket balls. Molten lead was dropped from the top of the tower into cold water, solidifying in perfectly spherical shape. You can climb the internal spiral staircase to the very summit for a shot-putter's view of the countryside.

A complex of modern glass office buildings at **Kingston** is the working headquarters for Australia's extensive operations in the neighbourhood of the South Pole. The Antarctic Division of the Department of Science and Technology coordinates the logistics and the research in fields such as glaciology, botany, physics and medicine. Inside the main building are displays of sleds and faded flags from pioneering expeditions. Australia maintains four permanent stations in the Antarctic.

LAUNCESTON

Tasmania's second city is an agreeable, roomy town at the head of the Tamar River. Launceston exudes an unexpected Englishness: elm trees, rose bushes and patriotic statues and plaques. The trip north from Hobart skirts soft green hills studded with sheep. In the villages, to enliven the scene, the

---

Apple Country

With its temperate climate, Tasmania is famous for its apples, which have been exported for more than a century. For all the juicy details, you can visit the apple museum in the farming and fishing town of Dover, south of Hobart.

One of the greatest names in apples is Tasmanian. Granny Smith—formally Mrs. Maria Smith—was the "inventor" of a versatile apple. The Granny Smith is good for eating as well as cooking, and can be stored over a long period. Like many good things, it was an accident. Seeds from some Tasmanian crab apples sprouted in Mrs. Smith's garden, and she nursed them into trees from which a new species of green apple was developed. Every Granny Smith apple grown anywhere in the world is a descendant of her original seedlings. A memorial honours Granny Smith in the Sydney suburb of Eastwood, where she lived.

Sweet-smelling lavender harvested by machine.

houses have roofs the colour of fire engines.

Launceston was founded in 1805 as Patersonia. Soon afterwards, the name was changed to that of the town of Launceston in Cornwall, birthplace of the colony's governor. The historic aspects of the town are enthusiastically preserved, starting in the very centre, the **City Square.** This ensemble challengingly groups together a modern pyramid-style state office building, a Japanese garden, and a building from 1830, **Macquarie House.** Restored to mint condition, this sometime warehouse, barracks and office building now serves as part of the local museum.

The main building of the **Queen Victoria Museum,** a short stroll away on Wellington Street, has something for everyone, from stuffed platypuses to blunderbusses, from prisoners' chains to an invigorating collection of modern art. One surprising attraction here is an intact **joss house** which originally served the Chinese tin miners in the Tasmanian town of Weldborough. The temple, rich in intricate gold leaf effects, was called the southernmost working joss house in the world. Visitors can discover the mysteries of the Southern night sky in the **planetarium.**

Life in early 19th-century Tasmania is recaptured in the **Penny Royal** development. A cornmill built in 1825 has been reconstituted, and a cannon foundry and arsenal created to demonstrate the stages of gunpowder manufacture from the distillation of saltpetre to the finished

cannonballs. By way of quality control you can shoot a cannon. Other attractions here are a paddle steamer, a naval sloop and an ancient tramcar.

Just around the bend is the **Cataract Gorge**, a stirring geological feature, and it's within walking distance of the centre of town. Here the South Esk River slices between steep cliffs on its route to the Tamar. There are hiking trails, boating opportunities, and, for sightseers who don't suffer queasy spells, a chairlift spanning the canyon from on high.

PORT ARTHUR

Although it evokes melancholy memories, the most visited historic highlight of Tasmania is the old penal colony of Port Arthur, only an hour's drive from Hobart. The relics are

187

deemed so important they're protected by the National Parks and Wildlife Service.

Port Arthur was founded in 1830 as the place to punish convicts in the second degree. Having been exiled to Tasmania for a first crime, some of the prisoners were convicted of new crimes on the spot. These really hopeless cases would be sent to Port Arthur as the last resort. Tough discipline was common in all penal institutions at that time, but Port Arthur acquired a reputation as an exceptionally brutal scene. Chain gangs, encouraged by the lash, built the

Incorrigible yet nostalgic, convicts built a little bit of England on the other side of the world.

solid stone buildings which have survived more than a century of abandonment, fire, storm and looting.

The biggest building still standing, four storeys high, was designed to be a storehouse but became a penitentiary for 650 inmates. Other surviving buildings are the lunatic asylum and, next door, the "model" prison. Both have been restored. Convicts designed and built a large church, now in ruins. Its 13 spires represent Christ and the apostles. Then there is the mortuary, which did a lively business; more than 1,700 graves occupy the nearby Isle of the Dead. Other than that, Port Arthur was almost escape-proof, with sharks waiting on one side and killer dogs on the other. In all, some 10,000 prisoners did time at Port Arthur during its 47 years of operation.

WILDERNESS

For many Australians from the other side of the Bass Strait, Tasmania is the closest they can get to European-style scenery. This far from Europe, though, the landscape is almost untouched by civilization. One good reason it's unspoiled: it's often unapproachable by road. Four-wheel-drive vehicles, canoes, rafts, or just sturdy legs are the best ways of penetrating these wild places.

In Tasmania a higher percentage of the total area has been set aside as national parks than in any other state.

South West National Park covers nearly all of the south-western corner of Tasmania: rugged mountains, glacial lakes, icy rivers and forests of giant Antarctic beeches. One recent feature is the new Lake Pedder, flooded to 25 times its natural size for a hydroelectric project. For better or worse, the controversial scheme brought the first roads to the area.

Cradle Mountain–Lake St. Clair National Park, a few hours drive north-west of Hobart, is a savage wonderland of mountain peaks and waterfalls, temperate rainforests, and lakes astir with trout. The wildlife is all around: wallabies, possums, Tasmanian devils and wildcats. If the Tasmanian tiger wasn't thought to be extinct, this would probably be the place to find one.

Mount Field National Park, just an hour's drive from Hobart, is popular in winter as an easy-to-reach, no-fuss skiing area. In summer the heathlands beyond the giant forests break out in alpine flowers, though some areas are covered with pesky thickets of horizontal scrub, a Tasmanian speciality. At the entrance to the national park is a village with the engaging name of National Park.

189

WHAT TO DO

SPORTS

The sporting life in Australia is inescapable, from the dawn jogger puffing past your window to the football crowds celebrating late into the night with shouting, songs and car horns. In a country so beautiful, with a climate so benign, you'll be tempted to join the crowds... playing the game yourself or watching the professionals. Under the dependable sun, everything is possible, from skiing—on water or snow—to surfing to sailing.

Sport, it's often said, is a passion Down Under. You can measure its impact by the newspapers, with their staggeringly comprehensive sports sections, and the television, which seems to devote half its time to live sports coverage and a lot of the rest to the results. If Australians are not playing a game or watching it, they're most likely betting on the result, or at least arguing about it.

In what other country could a racehorse be so revered as Phar Lap, winner of the 1930 Melbourne Cup? When he died, after a heroic victory in the United States, flags flew at half mast in Sydney. Today Phar Lap's body is the star attraction in Melbourne's National Museum, and his mighty heart is preserved in the Institute of Anatomy in Canberra. The race itself brings the nation to a temporary halt as everyone tunes in to listen.

Tastes change. More than a century ago, a guide book gloomily reported that very little hunting was available around Sydney, except when "occasionally parties are made up for rabbit, wallaby or kangaroo shooting". In 1903 the first car race was run in Australia. Three years later, daringly, surf bathing in the daytime became legal in Sydney. Water-skiing caught on in 1936. Australia won the Davis Cup in 1939. Melbourne held the Olympic games in 1956, and Aussie athletes seized 35 of the medals. The world was becoming aware of Australia as a foremost sporting power, a nation of hardy, aggressive competitors who became champions in fields as varied as tennis and swimming, cricket and golf. In 1983 joyous delirium greeted the news that the yacht *Australia II*, with a revolutionary winged keel, had captured the America's Cup. Hitherto a bolted-down fixture of the New York Yacht Club, the silver cup went on show behind bulletproof glass in the Royal Perth Yacht Club, shining brightly, like the local pride.

Water Sports

Australia's endless coastline provides enough beaches, coves and ports to keep the nation in the swim all year round. If that isn't enough, there are lakes, rivers and swimming pools, Olympic size and backyard versions. Water sports of every variety are there for the taking.

Swimming in the Indian Ocean, the Tasman Sea or the Coral Sea is the sort of sport you'll long remember. But the surf can be as dangerous as it is invigorating. Most of the popular beaches are delineated by flags showing where it's safe to bathe. Beware of undertow or shifting currents and always obey the instructions of lifeguards. Sharks are a problem in some areas; when a shark alert is sounded, beat a retreat to the shore and ask questions later. In spite of their mild-sounding name, jellyfish are a very serious seasonal danger, especially in the north; elsewhere there may be Portuguese men-of-war, sea snakes or other silent menaces. Check locally before you put a foot in the surf. And a final word of caution: before you stretch out on the beach, protect yourself from the sun, which is more powerful than you think. Light

Amazingly transparent, a cool mountain stream in Northern Queensland.

complexions are particularly vulnerable to quick, painful sunburn and worse.

Snorkelling brings you into intimate contact with a brilliant new world of multicoloured fish and coral. The sport requires a minimum of equipment—a mask and breathing tube and, optionally, flippers to expand your range of operations. Almost anyone can learn how to do it in a matter of minutes; no great skill or stamina is required.

Scuba diving with an air tank is the graduate version of snorkelling. The best place in Australia for scuba outings—and quite possibly the best place in the world—is the coral wonderland of the Great Barrier Reef. Some of the resort islands are equipped for all the needs of divers, though you may have to supply your own regulator and demand valves. If you want to learn the sport, some resorts have weekly courses starting in the swimming pool or a quiet cove, leading up to an Open Water Certificate. Elsewhere along Australia's coasts, serious scuba divers devote themselves to exploring submerged wrecks.

Surfing. Yet another discovery by the intrepid Captain Cook, who came upon this sport in Hawaii. He wrote: "The boldness and address with which we saw them perform these difficult and dangerous manoeuvres was altogether astonishing and scarce to be credited." It was nearly two centuries before the first world championships were held in Sydney. Surfboard riding areas are marked by signs, flags or discs. The best-known surfing zone in the country must be Sydney's Bondi Beach, but there are many more choice locations up and down the coast of New South Wales. Although Queensland's Surfers Paradise may be just that, many experts prefer the giant rollers farther north at Noosa. Victoria's most popular surfing area is around Torquay. On the west coast, there are easily accessible surfing beaches near Perth and Bunbury.

Boating. Visiting yachts and their crews always get a warm Aussie welcome. At popular resorts, for instance along the Gold Coast or the Great Barrier Reef, sailing boats and powerboats can be chartered, with or without a professional skipper. Inland, you can command a sailing boat or a houseboat on the relaxing Murray River. Or you might just settle for an hour's hire of a pedal boat.

Fishing. You'll need a licence to fish inland waters in some states, but the sea is free for all amateurs. Outstanding trout

Parasailers prepare their maiden voyage at Surfers Paradise.

Champions Galore

Australia has produced so many sporting heroes that no hall of fame could hold them all. But as a reminder here's a rundown of some of the internationally celebrated names of modern times.

Tennis: *Frank Sedgman, Ken Rosewall, Lew Hoad, Rod Laver, Roy Emerson, Evonne Goolagong, Margaret Court.*

Golf: *Jim Ferrier, Peter Thompson, David Graham, Greg Norman.*

Swimming: *John Marshall, Dawn Fraser, Shane Gould.*

Cricket: *Don Bradman, Greg Chappell, Dennis Lillee, Rodney Marsh.*

Track Events: *John Landy, Herb Elliott, Ron Clarke.*

Motor racing: *Jack Brabham, Alan Jones, Peter Brock.*

All is silence, but for birdsong and the footfall of intrepid joggers.

fishing is found in Tasmania and the Snowy Mountains. Seasons and bag limits vary with the district. As for game fishing, the challenge of the giant black marlin is best met off the northern coast of Queensland. If your catch weighs less than half a ton, it's polite to throw the little fellow back. Or settle for tuna, mackerel or sailfish. Good deep-sea fishing is also found off the coast of Western Australia, especially at Geraldton, and in the Spencer Gulf, near Adelaide. In the north, a coveted game fish is the barramundi, a great fighter prized for its delicate flesh.

Sports Ashore

Golf. The landscaping may be foreign, the climate may be a better year-round bet than you're accustomed to, but the game's the same. Melbourne considers itself the nation's golfing capital, with championship courses like Victoria and the Royal Melbourne. All the cities have golf clubs; they often operate under exchange agreements with clubs overseas, or you may have to be introduced by a local member. With no formality at all you can hire a set of clubs and play at one of the public courses found in all the sizeable towns. Golf is also

a popular spectator sport in Australia. The Australian Open takes place in November.

Tennis. Having produced so many illustrious tennis champions, Australia takes the game seriously. You'll find courts available in the towns and resorts; some hire out rackets and shoes. If you're just watching, join the crowd. The biggest throng ever to watch a Davis Cup match was counted in Sydney in 1954: more than 25,000 fans. The world's top tennis stars usually tour Australia in December and January.

Bowling (lawn bowls). All around Australia this leisurely sport finds men and women in cream-coloured costumes spending hours in the sun decorously bowling on neatly trimmed grass. If you're a bowler you'll be able to find a game at almost any club. If you're just sightseeing, spare a few minutes to absorb the restful scene.

Skiing. Although Australia doesn't claim to have invented skiing, fur trappers in Tasmania were getting around on something similar to skis in the 1830s. The season in the Australian Alps usually lasts from June to September, sometimes into November, which should be inducement enough for skiers from the northern hemisphere. The best-known and best-equipped resorts in the Snowy Mountains include

195

Aussies love horses and betting more than almost anything.

Thredbo Village, Perisher Valley and Smiggin Holes (N.S.W.) and Mt. Buller, Falls Creek, Mt. Hotham and Mt. Buffalo (Victoria). What's claimed to be the longest chairlift in the world runs 6 kilometres (3½ miles) above Thredbo. It can take more than an hour to reach the top.

The "Footy" Craze

In Australia the subject of **football** is so vast and complex—for a start, four different kinds of football are played—that the stranger is likely to be left gasping on the sidelines. But since the country is crazy about it, a few definitions, at least, may be useful. Incidentally, whatever type of football is being discussed, the fans are likely to call it "footy".

Australian Rules Football, the

most exotic of the games from a foreigner's viewpoint, was introduced in Melbourne in 1858. Its zone of influence is mostly Melbourne and the south. Crowds of 100,000 and more come out to watch the finals in September, which generate the excitement of an American Super Bowl or an English FA Cup Final. The sport, combining elements of rugby, Gaelic football and other forms of the game, is characterized by long-distance kicks and passes and high scoring on an oversized but crowded field—with 18 players to a side.

Rugby League, the professional, international version of the sport, is played mainly in Sydney and Brisbane. It's a roughhouse game offering great physical challenges to the players, 13 to a side.

Rugby Union, with teams of

15, is fast, rough and engrossing to the fans. Players from private schools add a posh aura to the violence of the tackles.

Soccer is the oldest of the games. In Australia it has benefited from the more recent waves of immigrants, and most clubs have ethnic connections. While soccer commands the biggest crowds in Europe and South America, its Australian audience is relatively restrained.

More Sports to Watch

Australians have been playing **cricket** since the early days of the penal colony at Sydney Cove. Purists deplore the innovations they've inflicted on it recently, but there's no stopping progress. In its traditional form, the game goes on interminably—for as long as five days. In the television age the Aussies have had the temerity to make a show-biz spectacle out of a gentlemanly pursuit, playing at night under the lights in gaudy uniforms and ending the match decisively in a single day. Fortunately for conservative fans, the old-fashioned Test survives as well under the Australian sun. The season extends from October to the end of March.

Horse racing. Almost every Australian town, even in the Outback, has a race track, and the big cities have more than one. Saturdays and holidays are the best times to go to the races. Betting on horses, or most other things, is as Australian as ice-cold beer. Enthusiasts who can't make it to the race can participate in their own way through off-track betting facilities, legal and computerized and called TAB for Totalizator Agency Board. For punters who prefer to patronize illegal bookmakers, they, too, operate wherever races are run. The biggest race of the year is the Melbourne Cup, a 2-mile classic so obsessional that the day it is run—the first Tuesday in November—is a legal holiday in Victoria. This is just as well, for nothing would get done in any case while the state has horses on the brain.

Trotting (harness racing) can be seen in big cities and some provincial locations. In the capital cities the trotters run under floodlights. Some of the stakes are enormous.

Greyhound racing is another spectacle that draws crowds of betters. Spurred to speed by the unfulfillable promise of an artificial rabbit, the dogs usually run in the cool of the evening; the audience can be as fascinating as the sport itself.

Motor racing. Big races take place near Brisbane, Sydney and Melbourne. The biggest of all is the Australian Grand Prix, at which many of the world championship contenders compete.

ENTERTAINMENT

Australia has never been known as a prim and priggish place, so it should come as no great shock that a lot of racy entertainment is available. What may surprise you, though, is the rich variety of "heavyweight" cultural attractions: opera, ballet, concerts, drama. Between the extremes there's something for everybody who just wants a relaxing evening out. Most of the towns have a "what's on" magazine or brochure listing details on the local agenda all the way from art exhibitions to X-rated excesses.

Theatre has been going strong in Australia for a couple of centuries. In 1789, scarcely a year after New South Wales was founded, a troupe of convicts put on a Restoration comedy *(The Recruiting Officer)* by George Farquhar to help celebrate the birthday of King George III. The first real theatre opened in Sydney in 1796. Drama today is at its liveliest in Sydney and Melbourne, where professional companies produce performances of the classics, recent British or American hits, and locally written plays. Some of the theatres themselves are works of art—architectural classics from a more opulent age, or modern showplaces. A typically Australian variation on the theatrical theme is the pub-theatre or theatre-restaurant, where dinner is served before or along with a cabaret, satirical review or musical comedy.

Opera has attracted enthusiastic audiences Down Under since the days of Dame Nellie Melba. In modern times the coloratura brilliance of Dame Joan Sutherland has spread her fame, and that of Australia, around the world. Seeing grand opera in the Sydney Opera House made a gala occasion even more so; but opera-goers in other cities have their consolation in the way of acoustics and atmosphere in their newer theatres.

Ballet. The country's prime classical dance company, the Australian Ballet, founded in 1962, is based in Melbourne but spends nearly half its time performing in Sydney. Among the foremost modern dance troupes are the Sydney Dance Company and the Australian Dance Theatre.

Concerts. When it comes to classical music, the paramount patron of the arts is the Australian Broadcasting Commission (ABC), which operates a symphony orchestra in each state capital. These orchestras crisscross the country, bringing live, serious music to small towns as well as the great concert halls. The ABC also keeps up a steady stream of good recorded music on its ABC-FM network. Another influential promoter of serious music, called Musica Viva Australia, specializes in chamber concerts.

Jazz in Australia can be as traditional or avant-garde as you like. In the big cities there are jazz clubs, where you might hear a visiting immortal or an up-and-coming local band, and pubs featuring jazz, perhaps on weekends only. Indoor and outdoor jazz concerts are also advertised.

Other music—folk, pop, rock or beyond—can reveal something of a nation's soul. Listen to a bearded troubadour dishing out bush ballads in an Outback saloon, or catch one of the flashy new groups rocking in the footsteps of such Australian "greats" as the Seekers, the Bee Gees, AC/DC and Men at Work.

Nightlife in the big cities flourishes in conventional nightclubs, discos and musical pubs. Then there are the private clubs which provide all-round entertainment for their members; overseas visitors are usually admitted with a flash of a passport, but the dress regulations may be more formal than you would have expected. The clubs in many areas pay their way through the profits of their slot machines, called poker machines (more affectionately pokies), which provide endless fascination for Australians. For punters who prefer to wager folding money, gambling **casinos** are available in big cities and resorts. Usually open very late into the night, they are equipped for, among other pursuits, roulette, craps, keno, blackjack, baccarat and the backwoods game of two-up (see p. 138) in a more refined, electronic version.

Cinema. The Australian film industry, founded at the end of the 19th century, has contributed more than its share to the art of moving pictures, taking a great leap forward in the 70s to become one of the most important national cinemas. Some of the big ones of modern times —*Picnic at Hanging Rock, My Brilliant Career, Breaker Morant,* the *Mad Max* series, *Crocodile Dundee*—have given the world a look at Australia's scenery as well as some insight into the national character and preoccupations. In spite of the inroads of television and home video, multi-screen cinemas are going strong, in the town centres as well as the suburbs. The big cities also have specialized cinemas for art films, foreign films and revivals.

Jazzy jam session echoes round the Rocks in Sydney.

Festivities

Not many tourists would plan their whole trip to coincide with the begonia festival in Ballarat, the Bendigo bonsai exhibition, or even the crazy dry-river regatta in Alice Springs. But knowing when and where the special events are scheduled might add that extra splash of local colour to your holiday.

January: *Sydney* Festival, a month of concerts, drama, exhibitions, sports and special events. *Perth* Cup horse racing classic at Royal Ascot Racecourse. *Hahndorf, South Australia* Schuetzenfest. *Nationwide* Australia Day holiday.

February: *Hobart* Royal Regatta. *Perth* Festival, sporting and cultural events. *Melbourne* Victorian Open golf championships.

FESTIVITIES

March and April: *Ballarat, Victoria* Begonia Festival, flower displays and artistic events. *Melbourne* Moomba, carnival with parades, fireworks, sports events, cultural attractions. *Adelaide* Festival of Arts (even-numbered years), three weeks of opera, ballet, theatre, art and literary events. *Canberra* Festival, pop concerts, fairs, flypasts. *Barossa Valley, South Australia* Vintage Festival, celebrating the wine harvest (odd-numbered years) with German-Australian gaiety. *Sydney* Royal Easter Show, Sydney Showgrounds, Australia's largest country fair. Sydney Cup Week, a pageant of horse racing.

May: *Alice Springs* Bangtail Muster, rodeo extravaganza. Camel Cup. *Adelaide* Cup horse race and associated festivities (a legal holiday locally).

June: *Darwin* Beer Can Regatta, in which all the boats are ingeniously constructed of used beer cans. *Perth and beyond* Western Australia Week, commemorating the state's original settlement with cultural and sporting events. *Brisbane* Cup, horse race.

July: *Gold Coast, Queensland* Marathon. *Melbourne* Grand National Steeplechase. *Darwin* Show, agricultural exhibition.

August and September: *Brisbane* Royal National Show, agricultural roundup with animals, fireworks and fun. *Mt. Isa, Queensland* Rodeo, Australia's biggest. *Alice Springs* Henley-on-Todd Regatta, bottomless boats racing hilariously on a waterless riverbed. *Thredbo, New South Wales* Ski championships, Snowy Mountains. *Adelaide* Royal Show, South Australia's agricultural summit meeting. *Melbourne* Royal Show, ten days of bucolic attractions, sports competitions and amusements. *Townsville, Queensland* Pacific Festival, cultural and artistic events with strong Aboriginal participation. *Toowoomba, Queensland* Carnival of Flowers, floral parade and gardening competitions. *Various capital cities* Australian Rules football finals. *Brisbane* Warana festival, floats, bands, concerts.

October: *Perth* Royal Show, state fair with animals, farm equipment and sideshows. *Hobart* Royal Show, Tasmanian agricultural exhibition. *Bowral, New South Wales* Tulip Time, display of spring flowers. *McLaren Vale, South Australia.* Wine Bushing Festival, celebrating vines and wines. *Adelaide* Australian Formula 1 Grand Prix.

November: *Melbourne* Victorian Spring Racing Carnival, culminating in the nation's biggest, highest-stake race, the Melbourne Cup. *Adelaide, Melbourne, Perth* Golf tournaments.

December: *Perth* Australian Derby, horse race. *Sydney to Hobart* Yacht Race and *Tasmanian* Fiesta, carnival and sports competitions.

SHOPPING

First, the cautionary note: don't expect to wallow in bargains in Australia; the production costs are too high. Now the good news: the shopping is gratifying and varied, whether it's accompanied by a murmur of big-city sophistication or the homespun twang of Outback simplicity.

In most cities, browsers and window-shoppers congregate along the pedestrian malls. Department store chains like David Jones, Grace Bros. and Myer provide a dependable cross-section of what's available. And the downtown arcades and courts are crammed with boutiques handling everything from high fashion to silly souvenirs.

In Sydney the skyscrapers have subterranean shopping arcades; the principal pedestrian plaza, Martin Place, is not a shopping mall at all but a perfect place to relax between sorties. In Melbourne the main shopping streets are Collins and Bourke, and the Bourke Street Mall is the heart of the matter; some Melbourne arcades are historic architectural sites. Rundle Street Mall is the essence of shopping in Adelaide, and traffic-free Hay Street Mall is Perth's sprawling equivalent.

Shopping hours usually run nonstop from 8.30 or 9 a.m. to 5 or 5.30 p.m., Monday to Friday, and Saturday mornings until noon. One night a week, either Thursday or Friday depending on the city, the stores stay open until about 9 p.m. In some places, tourist needs are catered for on Sundays, as well.

What to Buy

The temptations are as diverse as mass-produced knick-knacks and works of art. As anywhere else, it all depends on your taste and your budget. Here's a brief survey of the distinctive shopping possibilities to keep in mind as you travel across Australia. The categories are arranged in alphabetical order.

Aboriginal arts and crafts. The Northern Territory and North Queensland are good places to come across authentic boomerangs, didjeridus (drone pipes) and works of art, but you can find Aboriginal products in specialist stores all over the country. Outback artists produce traditional paintings on bark, the subjects and style recalling the prehistoric rock paintings: kangaroos, emus, fish, snakes, crocodiles, and impressions of tribal ceremonies. Other Aboriginal painters use modern materials to produce canvases in a style that looks uncannily like some abstract-expressionist work, yet recounting Dreamtime legends and rituals. If the themes are old, the economics are contemporary; the price tags on paintings may go into four figures. Fine workmanship is also seen on some of the painted wood sculptures of animals and birds. You'll see large, brightly decorated didjeridus, wind instruments made from tree trunks hollowed out by obliging termites. More portably, there are clap-sticks for percussion accompaniment. Aboriginal craftsmen also produce decorated wooden shields and, inevitably, boomerangs. The better boomerangs, hand carved and painted, can be quite expensive. Aboriginal craftsmen also create rather pricey trinkets such as baskets and place-mats from pandanus leaves.

Antiques might seem a fruitless field in a country as young as Australia, but some worthy colonial pieces turn up: furniture, clocks, jewellery, porcelain, silverware, glassware, books and maps. Some dealers specialize in non-Australian antiques, for instance Chinese ceramics or Japanese screens. In Sydney the Paddington district is full of antique shops. Melbourne's antique centre is High Street, Armadale.

Diamonds. In recent years the thinly populated Kimberly region of Western Australia has been the site of a whopping big diamond strike. The cut and polished results of this bonanza —precious stones in yellow, brown or white, but especially pink—are sold at jewellers in the major cities.

Duty-free shopping is highly organized throughout Australia, not just at airports but in the cities. Some downtown duty-free stores claim to have lower prices and greater variety than the airport shops. If you're in the market for a Japanese stereo rig or camera, not to mention the familiar spirits and perfume options, the competition among duty-free firms has made Australia an interesting marketplace. You have to produce your air ticket and passport at the duty-free store. You mustn't open the packages before you leave the country; on your departure you have to show them to the customs agent, who'll be looking for you.

Fashions. Sunny Australia is a good place to pick up resort fashions, though the prices are almost always at high-season peaks. The swimwear, pareus, shorts and T-shirts come in novel patterns, likely to excite admiration at other latitudes. A most unusual design in fancy shirts is sold at the historic Hyde Park Barracks in Sydney: pin-stripes with, at the bottom, the broad arrow symbol of a prisoner of King George III.

Hats. You, too, can go home in a digger hat, the kind with a chin-strap and one side of the brim up, as worn by Breaker Morant and his ANZAC mates. Or one of the cowboy-style hats that protect Australian stockmen from sun and rain. Then there is the jokey cork hat, with dangling wine corks to discourage the attentions of those vexatious Outback flies.

Kangaroo-skin products include toy kangaroos and koalas and other such souvenirs, some of them quite trite. The cheapest stuffed kangaroos and koalas, sometimes wrapped in patriotic Australian packaging, are imported.

Opals lie embedded in the most ordinary rocks until somebody stumbles on them. Australia produces the great majority of all the world's opals. Precious opals come in three sorts, primarily from fields in three

states. Coober Pedy, in South Australia, the continent's biggest opal field, produces the white, or milky, opal. In the Outback of Queensland, around Quilpie, the reward is the so-called boulder opal, with brilliant colours and patterns. Finally, Lightning Ridge in New South Wales is the source of black opals (more blue than black), the most expensive of all. You could go to the opal fields to find a stone of your own, simply noodling through the hills of rejected rocks. It's easier to buy an opal at one of the specialist stores in any of the cities. Opals, considered among Australia's best buys, are sold unset or as finished jewellery. The big jewellery shops can arrange tax-free purchase for foreign visitors, but you'll have to pay duty when you arrive home.

Outback clothing. Australian city folk sometimes like to affect the kind of fashions the stockmen (cowboys) wear, and you, too, might want to try a bit of ruggedness-by-association. There are flannel shirts, moleskin (a durable form of cotton) trousers, kangaroo-hide belts, oilskin coats to withstand any squall, and low- or high-heeled boots to strut in.

Paintings and prints by con-

temporary Australian artists are on show in commercial galleries in many areas, but the biggest concentration is in the big cities. Sydney galleries are clustered in the central shopping district and in Paddington. In Melbourne try the City, Toorak Road, and High Street, Armadale. They'll handle the packing, insurance and shipping for you.

Sheepskin. With sheep out-

Aboriginal artefacts or trendy trinkets—Australian creations should be top of your list.

numbering people by about ten to one, it's only logical that sheepskin products are available all over Australia, and usually at good prices. If it isn't too hot to think about such things, look over the sheepskin boots, hats, coats, rugs and novelty items.

Souvenirs, ingenious or hackneyed, indigenous or imported, pop up everywhere you travel, in cities, resorts and along the way at roadside stands. Tourists seem unable to resist miniature kangaroos, koalas and, in Tasmania, almost-lovable Tasmanian devil dolls. Plastic boomerangs and beer-can holders head the very long list of less artistic souvenirs, followed by saucy T-shirts.

Tasmanian timber. Huon pine grows for centuries before it gets big enough to interest Tasmania's lumbermen. Eventually this long-lasting, fine-grained, fragrant wood is carved into furniture, bowls, egg-cups, candlesticks … even rolling-pins. Or you can take home a sachet of the shavings, suitable for sniffing when you're feeling nostalgic for Tassie.

Woollen goods. Those sheep again: look for high-quality sweaters and scarves, and tapestries, too. You can also buy hand-spun wool.

Sydney's Strand Arcade has become a classic landmark.

EATING OUT

Australian cooks certainly merit an honourable mention or two in the international gastronomic competition. After all, the resources they enjoy are wonderfully wholesome. The beef, lamb, seafood and vegetables are mouthwatering.

And if you want to gild the lily with an exotic sauce, the immigrant community has contributed a repertoire of spices and subtleties to satisfy sophisticated requirements. A smattering of foreign food has filtered down to the most insular Aussies; the blackboard of a backwoods café may well list moussaka and spaghetti bolognese, or something as dizzily eclectic as "dim sims with chips".

Australians everywhere eat well, and, at least in the big cities, with some refinement. The quantities, which match the continent's size, help to explain some of the potbellies you'll notice straining T-shirts. This is ironic when you consider the gaunt profiles of the first settlers, who barely endured when the crops failed and the livestock died or wandered into the bush. Survival rations were issued; stealing food became a capital offence. As the settlers struggled against famine, the Aborigines, Stone Age hunter-gatherers, watched with detachment. Their own traditional diet was crammed with proteins and vitamins, thank you.

If you're around Alice Springs you can sample an Aboriginal delicacy, witchetty grubs, the larvae of beetles and moths found in trees and roots. In the bush they are eaten baked at best, raw if necessary. Some brave visiting gourmets say witchetty grubs have a rich, sweetish taste. Otherwise, Aborigines favour staples like roast wallaby, snake or lizard, preferably with a garnish of various grasses, fruits, seeds and berries.

Kangaroo has gone off the menu in restaurants over recent years, thanks to conservationist pressures and perhaps sneaking regrets about consuming the national symbol. But if it's unfamiliar meat you're craving, you might come across buffalo steak —marinated, highly seasoned, and tender as good beef.

What to Eat

Breakfast is anything you want it to be, from pastry and coffee to the endless buffets of fruits, eggs, meats and breads marshalled by the big hotels. If your early morning appetite is voracious enough to tackle some dinkum bush tucker, many a café can rustle up steak and eggs or lamb chop and eggs. You'll also be offered a few breakfast oddities: spaghetti on toast or baked beans on toast. All of which takes us more than halfway to lunch.

Fish and seafood. Whether it's a stand-up version of fish and chips or a candlelit restaurant's lobster à la spending spree, the harvest of Australia's tropical and temperate oceans offers the food-lover great variety and promise. Among the fine fish adorning the menu: delicious snapper (sometimes still spelled the German way, Schnapper), meaty John Dory, smallish flounder and bigger sole (they have both eyes on the same side, like a Picasso face), bony but flavoursome whiting (no relation to the English whiting), and tropical trevally. Then there's barramundi, which means "big scales" in an Aboriginal language, and is found in both fresh and salt water; game fishermen in the north take "barra" of up to 15 kilograms (33 pounds) and consumers relish its tender fillets. Along the Barrier Reef they even eat red emperor, a fish so gorgeous it might take a snorkeller's breath away.

Treat yourself to succulent seafood specialities like Sydney rock oysters, as delicious as any in the world, and Brisbane's famous Moreton Bay bug, a

Sumptuous array for a seaborne picnic.

crustacean to gloat over, and mud crabs, gloriously meaty. Lobster, grilled or thermidored, is for special occasions. You'll also come across some of the lobster's freshwater cousins, known locally as yabbies. Prices are less forbidding when it comes to steamed mussels or fried prawns.

Meat seems to boil down to grilled steaks and roast lamb or lamb chops, especially in the less elaborate restaurants. Meat pies are produced with regional differences; in Adelaide the crusty delight evolves into the beloved floater, a meat pie afloat in green pea soup (see p. 147). Incidentally, no matter what kind of steak you order it will arrive well-done unless you explain that you want it "rare"—in which case it may escape incineration, but not by much. If you feel strongly about rare meat, emphasize that you want it "blue". Otherwise, nothing but good can be said about Australian beef. If you're up to it, try carpetbag steak (stuffed with oysters). Apart from beef and lamb you'll find pork in the form of chops, roast, or spare ribs, and chicken. All sorts of meat are conducive to outdoor barbecuing, a favourite Australian pastime. You may also come across a distinctly Australian mixed salad, combining slices of cold meat and cheese with vegetables.

Fresh from the furrow, **vegetables** add flavour and wholesomeness to the largely meat-and-potato diet. If your taste buds have been benumbed by the banality of mass-produced vegetables elsewhere, you're in for pleasant surprises in Australia. But overcooking remains a hard habit to break.

Fruit from all the climatic zones grows in Australia. To name but a few: apples, cherries, plums and berries from the temperate latitudes, and avocados, bananas, papayas, passionfruit, pineapples and mangoes full of juicy tropical sweetness.

Desserts. Calorific cakes and fruit pies come in many tempting flavours. Also very rich is a favourite Australian dessert, the light and fluffy pavlova, a meringue concoction traditionally topped with kiwi fruit. It is named after Anna Pavlova, an immortal of the early 20th-century Russian ballet, who visited Australia on a world tour. On a similar cultural plane, peach melba, with ice cream and raspberry sauce, was dedicated to Melbourne's eponymous opera diva. The fruit-flavoured ice creams are delicious on their own.

The fate of Red Centre sheep is to end up as shish kebabs.

212

Foreign Food

The Australian melting pot cooks up some first-class ethnic specialities. Name a national cuisine, however obscure, and you can sample it somewhere Down Under. In Melbourne, which claims to have the third biggest Greek population in the world (after Athens and Salonika) you don't have to look very far to find some authentic *taramosalata, dolmades* and *souvlaki*. Sydney is so cosmopolitan you can choose from dozens of cultural strains, yielding anything from Arab *pita* and *falafel* to Yugoslavian *cevapcici*. Darwin is noted for its high percentage of immigrants and transients, so you can choose from various shades of Chinese cuisine plus Indonesian, Malaysian and all manner of European styles.

Yesterday's boat people are now dishing up Vietnamese spring rolls. In several cities the Asian influence is strong enough to support self-service establishments offering "Chinese and Asian Smorgasbord"; for a moderate set fee you can pile your plate as high as you like with Shanghai sautéed prawns and Thailand's sweet-and-sour *mee grob*. At lunchtime, Chinese *dim sum* restaurants are popular with their vast array of dumplings, buns and snacks, also known as *yum cha* (meaning simply "to drink tea" in Cantonese).

Australian Wines

It's been a long time since wine snobs turned up their cultivated noses at what used to be the rough-and-ready product of Australia's sun-roasted vineyards. Some truly distinguished wines have evolved, and the experts have to admit that the country's merest *vin du pays* is more than potable. Even the humble "kangarouge" that comes in a cardboard box (known as a cask) is comparable to the grade of wine served in a carafe in a French bistro, or an Italian trattoria's *fiasco*.

Knowing a good thing when they taste it, Australians drink twice as much wine per head as Americans or Britons. What's left over—something like 100 million litres—is exported to more than 80 countries.

The Australian interest in wine goes back a couple of centuries. The founder of the New South Wales colony, Captain Arthur Phillip, had his priorities right. One of the first projects he ordered in 1788 was the planting of vines at Sydney Cove. Because of factors like the damp and the sea breezes, the site (now part of Sydney's Botanic Gardens) was quite wrong for growing grapes, which developed "black spot", and the experiment failed. But in 1791 three acres of vines were successfully planted a few miles inland.

Rum, not wine, became the favourite drink under Governor Phillip's successor. Free-enterprising army officers enjoyed a monopoly on the staggeringly profitable sales of rum, and abuses were reported to London. So Captain William Bligh, the original hardliner of Bounty fame, was despatched to clean up Australia. Governor Bligh, who never made a lot of friends, was deposed in the Rum Rebellion of 1808, a mutiny led by one of the first wine-growers, John Macarthur.

When Australians got around to appreciating their own production, the demand was strongest for fortified wines like port and sherry. Much later the populace opened its heart to the

kind of still wines that complement a meal—the refreshment of a cool white, the satisfaction of a robust red. And then, in recent years, the experts moved in to upgrade the average wine and propel the best into the big leagues.

As you explore the world of wines Down Under, keep in mind that European terminology on the labels can be innocently deceptive. A Cabernet from New South Wales is likely to taste quite different from the South Australian equivalent, which, in turn, is a far cry from its French namesake. Likewise, an Australian Rhine Riesling wine might be unrecognizable to a taster from Germany. This is because the soil and climate are so markedly different. Australians take it all in their stride, and although many of them are knowledgeable about wine, few are pretentious. In egalitarian Australia, the only "class" difference is that the "masses" buy their wine by the cask (two-, four- or five-litre cartons) costing less than beer, and the "ruling class" chooses expensive bottles.

You needn't look for vintages. In most cases they are irrelevant, the crop and climate being just as good one year as another. The specific region, too, can be vague, as blending to taste is common. Wines are named either generically (burgundy or moselle, for instance) or according to the pedigree of the grape (say, the noble Pinot Noir or Chardonnay). The varietal names can get complicated, for instance when Cabernet-Sauvignon is blended with Shiraz to become Cabernet-Shiraz.

Wine is produced in every Australian state, even rainy Tasmania and the baking Northern Territory (where a small "chateau" holds forth on the edge of Alice Springs). The biggest producer is South Australia, of which the best-known wineries are found in the beautiful Barossa Valley and the Southern Vales. The most important wine-producing region of New South Wales is the Hunter Valley. In Victoria the Goulburn Valley and Murray Valley are strongest. And Western Australia's Swan Valley and Margaret River areas have made their mark.

White wine far outsells red in Australia, with sweetish sparkling wines particularly popular. The nation's vineyards also provide rosé and, by way of fortification, sherry, port, vermouth and brandy.

... And Beer

Australians have such a raging thirst that only an ocean of beer can slake it. But the brew has to be cold enough to freeze the teeth and taste-buds. The icy temperature is so vital that real fans demand deep-frozen glasses, or enclose their cold "tinnies" in insulated holders.

For some years the world has been let in on the secret of Australian beer, which is widely exported. Foster's lager has been the most highly publicized brand abroad. Other beers generate pronounced regional loyalties —for instance Swan Lager in Western Australia and Castlemaine XXXX (called simply "four-ex") in Queensland.

Australian beer, in the pilsner or lager stream, is stronger than its nearest equivalent in the U.S. or Britain, though some European brews contain even more alcohol.

At the bar the size of a draught beer varies according to the state. You'll come across a middy, a schooner, a pot, a five and a stubby. When in doubt, simply ask for a beer. You can't go wrong.

Other Refreshments

For a change from wine and beer, try some of the country's fruit drinks. They come canned in inventive combinations of flavours, for instance a mixture of orange and passionfruit juices. Less vitamin-laden, all the familiar fizzy soft drinks are available. And, if you run out of thirst-quenching ideas, you *can* drink the water.

BERLITZ-INFO

CONTENTS

A ACCOMMODATION (see also CAMPING, YOUTH HOSTELS)

Australia welcomes the traveller with every kind of accommodation from five-star palaces to austere economy-class rooms. The luxury end of the spectrum matches the most sumptuous world standards, in the rooms and suites as well as the associated restaurants, lounges, saunas and spas. But even in budget-priced hotel and motel rooms you can expect a private shower or bath and toilet, a telephone, a TV set, a small refrigerator, and coffee- and tea-making equipment (and free coffee, tea and milk). In most areas air conditioning or at least a ceiling fan is provided.

There's no limit to the level of luxury a hotel or motel can attain, and either type can be anywhere—along the highway or right downtown. Distinguishing between the two can be confusing. The only sure difference is that a hotel has a bar open to the public—indeed, the most modest ones have little else to offer. "Hotel" and "pub" are synonymous. If a motel has a bar, it's usually strictly for the guests. So you cannot judge a hostelry by what it calls itself.

Private hotels, often small guest houses, do not have a licence for alcohol. There are Bed and Breakfast establishments—private homes taking paying guests—in towns or out on the farm. The big towns and resorts also have self-catering apartments with maid service and fully equipped kitchens, convenient for longer stays.

Overseas offices of Tourism Australia (the Australian Tourist Commission) have listings of hotels and motels. You can reserve accommodation through your travel agent, the nearest offices of the international and Australian hotel chains or your airline. Within Australia, the state tourist bureaus, domestic airlines and hotel chains offer instant, free bookings. If you arrive out of the blue, local tourist offices have desks for last-minute reservations.

Accommodation may be hard to find when Australians themselves go travelling by the million, during school holidays. These are staggered state by state but the crush periods are in May, August–September and from mid-December to the beginning of February.

AIRPORTS

The principal gateways are Melbourne, Sydney, Brisbane, Darwin and Perth. Other international airports serve Adelaide, Hobart, Townsville and Cairns. The domestic air network is very well developed, and even smallish towns usually have comfortable, efficient terminals. The biggest airports have the full range of restaurants and bars, newsstands, souvenir shops, post office and banks, and, in the case of Melbourne, a motel on the premises. The international airports have duty-free shops for both arriving and departing passengers. Free baggage carts are available.

Arriving passengers can travel from airport to town by taxi or bus. In Sydney, Brisbane, Adelaide, Darwin and Perth, airport bus service goes to and from the door of most hotels. Travel time ranges from 20 minutes (Perth and Darwin) to 40 minutes (Sydney).

Check-in time for departing passengers on domestic flights is 30 minutes before the scheduled flight time; international flights require check-in at least 90 minutes in advance.

CAMPING
Australians are avid campers, and you'll find campsites dotted all over the areas frequented by tourists. The sites tend to be jammed at school holiday times. They have at least the basic amenities, and in some cases much more in the way of comfort. Aside from roomy tents with lights and floors, some installations have caravans (trailers) or cabins for hire. Showers, toilets, laundry facilities and barbecue grills are commonly available. The national parks generally have well organized camping facilities; to camp beyond the designated zone you must ask the rangers for permission. There are coach tours for campers, or you can hire a campervan or motorhome by the day or week (see also CAR HIRE).

CAR HIRE
For seeing the Australian countryside at your own pace there's no substitute for a car. Brisk competition among the international and local car rental companies means you can often find economical rates or special deals, for instance unlimited mileage or weekend discounts. Rates are considerably higher if you drive in remote country areas. But in general it's worth shopping around.

In busy locations you can rent anything from a super-economy model or a four-wheel-drive vehicle to a limousine with or without chauffeur. Campervans and caravans (trailers) are available,

221

though most are reserved far in advance for school holiday periods.

To rent a car you'll need a current Australian, overseas or International Driver's Licence. The minimum age is 21, or in some cases 25. Third-party insurance is automatically included; for an additional fee you can also sign up for collision damage and personal accident insurance.

CHILDREN

Between the beaches and the bush, the kangaroos and the koalas, Australia will keep children amused and amazed. In addition to the natural beauties and oddities, the man-made attractions rate highly: boat excursions, vintage trains, imaginative amusement parks and "hands-on" museums.

In the great outdoors, too much sun can be debilitating. Be sure to supervise children at the beaches, where tides, sharks or poisonous jellyfish may be a menace. In the Outback, dangers can range from poisonous snakes and spiders to man-eating crocodiles. Seek local advice. On the "plus" side, the standard of hygiene is high everywhere.

If your hotel can't find someone to take care of your child, look in the yellow pages of the telephone directory under *Baby-sitters*.

CIGARETTES

Smokers can find a big selection of Australian and imported cigarettes on sale everywhere; they come in packs of 20, 25 or 30. Specialist shops also stock a plethora of imported cigars and pipe tobacco. Prices vary from state to state.

Smoking is prohibited on public transport, in theatres and elevators. Some hotels and restaurants have established smoke-free zones.

CLIMATE

The seasons, of course, are upside down: winter runs from June to August and Christmas comes in summertime. But it's much more complicated than that, for Australia covers so much ground, from the tropics to the temperate zone.

From November to March it's mostly hot, or at least quite warm, everywhere. In the north this period brings the rains, which can wash out roads and otherwise spoil vacation plans. In the south the nights, at least, are mild.

April to September is generally ideal in the tropics and central Australia—clear and warm. Occasional rain refreshes the south, with snow in the southern mountains.

By way of regional superlatives, Darwin is the state capital with the highest average hours of sunshine, but it also gets the most rain. Adelaide has the lowest average rainfall of all capital cities. Far to the south, Hobart is the coolest capital; its climate is similar to that of Britain. But statistics indicate that the cities of Australia bask in more sunshine than any others in the world.

For your guidance, here are some average daily maximum and minimum temperatures,* month by month, in degrees Fahrenheit:

		J	F	M	A	M	J	J	A	S	O	N	D
Sydney	max.	79	77	77	72	66	63	61	63	68	72	75	77
	min.	64	64	63	59	52	48	46	48	52	55	59	63
Brisbane	max.	84	84	82	79	73	71	68	72	75	79	82	84
	min.	69	68	66	61	55	52	48	50	55	61	64	63
Alice Springs	max.	99	97	91	84	73	68	66	72	79	88	93	95
	min.	72	71	64	57	48	43	41	45	50	59	64	68
Perth	max.	86	86	82	75	71	64	63	64	66	71	77	81
	min.	64	64	63	57	54	50	48	48	50	52	57	61

And in degrees Celsius:

		J	F	M	A	M	J	J	A	S	O	N	D
Sydney	max.	26	25	25	22	19	17	16	17	20	22	24	25
	min.	18	18	17	15	11	9	8	9	11	13	15	17
Brisbane	max.	29	29	28	26	23	21	20	22	24	26	28	29
	min.	21	20	19	16	13	11	9	10	13	16	18	17
Alice Springs	max.	37	36	33	29	23	20	19	22	26	31	34	35
	min.	22	21	18	14	9	6	5	7	10	15	18	20
Perth	max.	30	30	28	24	21	18	17	18	19	21	25	27
	min.	18	18	17	14	12	10	9	9	10	11	14	16

*Minimum temperatures are measured just before sunrise, maximum temperatures in the afternoon.

CLOTHING

You can forget your overcoat, but a sweater may come in handy, even in summer. After a hot day in the sun, the evening breeze can seem downright chilly. A light raincoat will serve in almost any season. Anywhere you go you'll need comfortable walking shoes and, in the Outback, a sunhat.

In cities like Melbourne and Sydney, businessmen wear suits and ties except on hot summer days, when they put on walking shorts with long socks. They still suffer neckties but abandon jackets. In less formal circumstances—sightseeing or shopping, for instance—both men and women wear shorts when it's warm. Some restaurants require jacket and tie, and even Outback restaurants and hotels may bar T-shirts and shorts in the evening.

COMMUNICATIONS

Australia's **post offices** are signposted "Australia Post". Most adhere to a 9-to-5 schedule Monday to Friday, though Sydney's General Post Office (GPO) also opens Saturday mornings. In Melbourne the GPO is open from 8 a.m. to 6 p.m. Monday to Friday with an after-hours counter as well. Hotels and souvenir shops also stock stamps. Letterboxes throughout Australia are red with horizontal white stripes.

If you don't know exactly where you'll be staying, you can have letters addressed to you c/o Poste Restante or the Post Office Delivery desk at the General Post Office in a city on your itinerary. You'll have to show identification when you pick up your mail.

Telephone. Telecom Australia runs more than 8 million telephones, at least 99 per cent of them linked to automatic exchanges. The network is highly sophisticated; from almost any phone, even in the Outback, you can dial anywhere in the country, and the signal is loud and clear. Many hotel rooms have phones from which you can dial cross-country (STD) or internationally (ISD). Some hotels add a surcharge to your telephone bill.

There are three kinds of public telephones. "Gold" phones, with a digital display, accept coins for direct-dial STD and ISD calls. The bulky, old-fashioned grey-green phones can also be used for local and long-distance calls. Red phones are for local calls only; put 20 cents in the slot.

Telephone directories give full instructions on dialling and details on emergency and other services.

Telegrams and **cablegrams** can be sent from any post office or dictated over the phone from your hotel or motel room. Most hotels have **telex** facilities, and **telefax** is increasingly available.

COMPLAINTS

As Australia has no special agency to deal with complaints, your best bet is to try to work out any problems face to face with the shopkeeper, hotel manager or whoever is involved.

COURTESIES (see also MEETING PEOPLE)

In Australia's egalitarian atmosphere, people usually introduce themselves by their first name, even in business relationships. They are punctual and will expect you to be the same.

Many areas of the country contain places or things that have special meaning to the Aborigines. These "sacred sites" are protected by law. Visitors should show consideration for their historical significance.

CRIME AND THEFT

As in most countries, it's wise to take precautions against burglary and petty theft. Check your valuables in the hotel's safe deposit box. Lock your room and your car. Be alert for pickpockets in crowded buses and markets.

Anti-drug laws vary greatly from state to state. Possession of 100 grams of cannabis or even less can mean up to two years in jail.

CUSTOMS, ENTRY AND EXIT REGULATIONS

All visitors except New Zealanders need valid passports and visas to enter Australia. Travel agencies and Australian consulates can provide visa application forms. The completed form, along with the passport and an identity photo, must be filed with the consulate. There is no charge for a visa. Only after a visa has been issued should you buy your air ticket. If you're arriving in Australia after a stop in an area where yellow fever is endemic, you must show a valid vaccination certificate.

Entry formalities. On the last leg of your flight to Australia you'll be asked to fill in a voluminous Customs form, swearing that you are not importing foreign foodstuffs, weapons, drugs or other forbidden articles. The checklist runs to 15 categories of prohibited items. There is also an Immigration form to fill in.

Even before you've disembarked from the aircraft you'll become aware of Australia's sensitivity about its unique environment, isolated from overseas pests and diseases. As seated passengers close their eyes, the passenger cabin is thoroughly sprayed to kill any insect stowaways. Once in the terminal you go through Quarantine, then Customs and Immigration. You'll have to show your return or onward ticket, and you may have to prove that you have sufficient funds for your stay. All the paperwork slows down the arrival procedure.

Duty-free. The chart below shows the main duty-free items you may take into Australia and, when returning home, into your own country:

Into:	Cigarettes	Cigars	Tobacco	Spirits	Wine
Australia	200	or 250 g.	or 250 g.	1 l.	or 1 l.
Canada	200	and 50	and 900 g.	1.1 l.	or 1.1 l.
Eire	200	or 50	or 250 g.	1 l.	and 2 l.
N. Zealand	200	or 50	or ½ lb.	1 qt.	and 1 qt.
S. Africa	400	and 50	and 250 g.	1 l.	and 2 l.
U.K.	200	or 50	or 250 g.	1 l.	and 2 l.
U.S.A.	200	and 100	and *	1 l.	or 1 l.
*A reasonable quantity					

Exit formalities. Leaving Australia, each passenger aged 12 or more must pay a $20 departure tax. (If you've run out of cash by then, major credit cards are accepted.) Children under 12 must obtain an exemption sticker from the Departure Tax counter, and proof of age is required. There is also a departure form to fill in for the Immigration authorities.

D DRIVING

Australia drives on the left. If you're not accustomed to it, you'll have to fight your reflexes all the time. Be specially vigilant when setting forth, at intersections, and after a break.

Australian roads are good, considering the size of the country and the problems of distance, terrain and climate. Although there are ever more freeways (expressways/motorways), some of them beautifully landscaped, most roads are two-lane highways, often overcrowded at busy times. In country areas you'll notice that cars usually have imposing extra bumpers designed to deflect kangaroos or other animals wandering onto the road. They may also have wire mesh screens to protect the windshield from gravel and stones launched by other vehicles on unpaved roads.

Regulations. Drive on the left and pass on the right. Drivers and passengers must wear seat belts. In some states there are on-the-spot fines for transgressors. The speed limit in cities and towns is normally 60 kilometres per hour (about 35 mph). In the country the limit in most states is 100 kmh (60 mph), but in South Australia and West Australia it's 110 kmh (65 mph). Driving under the influence of alcohol or drugs is a serious offence. Spot checks are made, with breath tests. In most states the limit on alcohol in the blood is .05 per cent, meaning in practice that three drinks will probably take you over the top.

City driving. Heavy traffic and parking problems afflict some of the downtown areas. Parking meters and "no standing" zones proliferate. For longer stays parking garages are the answer, but these, too, fill up. Melbourne's trams (streetcars) cause intriguing traffic problems. At a number of busy intersections, if you want to turn right you must do so from the *left* lane after the trams have passed, and when the cross-street light has turned green.

Outback driving (see also pp. 119–121). Always carry water. Fill up the fuel tank at every opportunity, for the next station may be a few hundred kilometres away. Some dirt roads are so smooth you may be tempted to speed, but the condition can change abruptly, and soft shoulders and clouds of dust are problems when other vehicles pass. Be extra cautious of road trains, consisting of three or four huge trailers barrelling down the highway pulled by a high-powered truck. Pass one, if you dare, with the greatest care.

Fuel. Many filling stations are open only during normal shopping hours, so you may have to ask where out-of-hours service is available. Petrol comes in regular and super grades and is dispensed by the litre. Many stations are self-service.

Road signs. All distances are measured in kilometres. Although most road signs are the standard international pictographs, many are written. Some of these will confuse even English-speakers:

Amphometer	**speed-measuring device complementing radar**
Crest	**steep hilltop limiting visibility**
Cyclist hazard	**dangerous *for* cyclists**
Dip	**severe depression in road surface**
Hump	**bump or speed-impeding obstacle**
Safety ramp	**uphill escape lane from steep downhill road**
Soft edges	**soft shoulders**

E ELECTRIC CURRENT

The standard everywhere in Australia is 240–250 volt, 50 cycle AC. Three-prong plugs, in the shape of a bird's footprint, are universal, so you should take an adaptor. Most hotel rooms also have 110-volt outlets for razors and small appliances. Otherwise, you'll need a voltage convertor.

EMBASSIES AND CONSULATES

The embassies or high commissions of some 70 countries are centred in Canberra, the national capital. They have consular sections dealing with passport renewal, visas and other formalities. Many countries also maintain diplomatic outposts—full-time or honorary—in the largest cities, which can be useful for citizens in difficulty. To find the address of your consulate, look in the white pages of the telephone directory under *Consuls* or in the yellow pages under *Consulates and Legations*.

EMERGENCIES

Ambulance—Fire—Police: Dial 000.
The 000 number—no coin required from public telephones—is in service in all cities and most towns. If you're in a remote area, however, look for the emergency numbers inside the front cover of the telephone directory. In the big cities there are round-the-clock dental emergency services as well as hospital emergency wards.

G

By Air

Flights from Asia, North America and Europe chiefly go to Sydney and Melbourne, but Australia has seven other international airports. Apex and other special fares reduce the expense of travelling such great distances. Only a knowledgeable travel agent can unravel the intricacies of these advance-booking fares, the prices depending on season and even the day of the week you choose. Look into round-the-world fares as well. Travel agents also have information on a big range of package tours available—fly-drive arrangements, rail or bus tours, camping vacations and safaris.

Getting to Australia by any route is a long haul. Average journey times: New York–Sydney 25 hours, Los Angeles–Sydney 19 hours, London–Sydney 24 hours, London–Perth 18 hours, Johannesburg–Perth 11 hours.

By Sea

Australian ports feature in the itineraries of a number of cruise ships. You can fly to, say, Bali or Fiji and embark on the liner there, sailing to Australia, then flying off from any Australian city, or resuming the cruise... around the world if you choose. Travel agents have cruise line schedules and brochures.

GUIDES

Guided tours are organized in all parts of the country, even in some small towns. Details are available at your hotel or the local tourist office.

HAIRDRESSERS AND BARBERS

H

There are unisex hairdressing salons for the sophisticates, or you can choose from more traditional segregated establishments, even old-fashioned, no-nonsense men's barber shops. Some beauty salons feature manicures, pedicures, facials, makeups and massage. Tipping is not a preoccupation in Australia, but a gratuity would not be refused.

HEALTH AND MEDICAL CARE

Standards of hygiene are high throughout Australia and, in fact, you can drink the tap water anywhere—unless a notice specifically

229

says otherwise. However, there are hazards in the countryside, starting with the threat of too much sun. Poisonous snakes and spiders lurk in many places, and bathers must beware of sharks and, in certain seasons and areas, dangerous jellyfish.

Australia has excellent medical services but the fees are high. Visitors are advised to arrange in advance for insurance to cover any medical or hospital costs on the trip.

If you have a doctor's prescription from your own physician abroad it cannot be filled by an Australian pharmacy unless you have it endorsed by a local doctor. As well as prescription drugs, Australian chemists sell toiletries, cosmetics and home remedies. In all the biggest cities at least one pharmacy operates 24 hours a day.

HITCH-HIKING

Although discouraged by the authorities, hitch-hiking is fairly commonplace in Australia, even in isolated spots where prospects are few. Successful practitioners recommend you show a sign with your destination clearly marked. It helps to choose a place where cars can pull over safely.

HOURS

Business hours vary slightly from place to place, but not as much as you might expect in a country with three time zones. Here are a few guidelines, subject to local variations.

Banks: 9.30 a.m. to 4 p.m. Monday to Thursday, till 5 p.m. Fridays. (But some big-city banks open earlier and close later for foreign currency exchange.)

Post office: 9 a.m. to 5 p.m. Monday to Friday.

Shopping: 8.30 or 9 a.m. to 5 or 5.30 p.m. Monday to Friday and from 9 to noon on Saturday. Each town has one late night per week when stores stay open until 8 or 9 p.m.

Offices: 9 a.m. to 5 p.m. Monday to Friday.

Bars/pubs/hotels: Licensing hours vary considerably from state to state and even hotel to hotel, but a typical schedule would be 10 a.m. to 10 p.m. Monday to Saturday, with some places permitting drinking after noon on Sundays. Nightclubs carry on until 2 a.m. or later.

Museums: 10 a.m. to 5 p.m. Monday to Saturday, noon to 5 p.m. Sundays.

Australian, a highly spiced version of the English language, is spoken everywhere in the nation. The vernacular is called *Strine*, which is the way the word "Australian" sounds in an extreme Australian pronunciation. The vocabulary is rich in inventive and amusing words spoken in what the uninitiated may take for a profound Cockney accent piped through the nose. Foreigners who listen carefully usually understand what's said, at least when it's repeated. The regional variations are insignificant.

Available in Australia is a wide selection of dictionaries and books, both erudite and jokey, delving into the derivation of local words and the unusual rhyming slang. But here, to tide you over, are a few dinkum Aussieisms:

abo	**Aborigine**
ace	**excellent**
back of beyond	**the Outback, remote area**
beaut	**beautiful, very good**
billabong	**water hole**
bush	**country area**
bushranger	**outlaw**
dinkum	**honest, authentic**
dinky-di	**the truth, genuine**
footy	**rugby-style football**
fossick	**to search, as for precious stones**
joey	**baby kangaroo**
Kiwi	**New Zealander**
mate	**good friend**
ocker	**a stereotypical Australian**
Oz	**Australia**
paddock	**field, often fenced**
Pom, Pommy	**English person**
roo	**Kangaroo**
station	**ranch**
tinny, or tube	**can of beer**
tucker	**food**
ute	**utility truck**
whinge	**to complain**

In addition to English a host of foreign languages serve the immigrant communities. Special multicultural radio stations broadcast in more than 50 languages. (See also RADIO AND TV.)

LAUNDRY AND DRY-CLEANING

Hotels and motels usually offer one-day laundry and dry-cleaning service for guests, but it can be quite expensive. Ask the receptionist, porter or maid. Many hotels and motels also have laundromat facilities on the premises.

LEGAL HOLIDAYS

Jan. 1	New Year's Day
April 25	Anzac Day
December 25	Christmas
December 26	Boxing Day (except S.A.)
Moveable dates:	Australia Day
	(Monday closest to 26 January)
	Good Friday
	Easter Eve
	Easter Monday
	Queen's Birthday

Other public holidays are celebrated only in certain states or a single region, for example Picnic Day in the Northern Territory in August, and Melbourne Cup Day in the metropolitan area in November. Still other holidays are marked at different times in different states: Wattle Day may be the first of August or September, depending on the state, and Labour Day comes any time between March and October, according to where you are.

LOST PROPERTY

If you've lost something, your hotel receptionist can probably tell you where to find the relevant Lost and Found department. In Sydney, for instance, there is one Lost Property Office for things lost in taxis, and another for property left behind in buses, trains and ferries. Otherwise, try the police.

M MAPS

State and local tourist offices give away useful maps of their areas. For more detailed maps, check at newsstands and bookstores. Car hire companies often supply free city directories showing each street and place of interest. For driving beyond the cities you'll want to buy an up-to-date road map of the region.

The maps in this book were prepared by Falk-Verlag, Hamburg.

MEETING PEOPLE

Australians are eminently approachable and convivial people, so you can strike up a conversation almost anywhere—at a bus stop, at the beach or in a pub. One way to get close to the people is to stay in Bed and Breakfast accommodation in family homes. Farmhouse vacations can also be arranged.

MONEY MATTERS

Currency: Since 1966, when pounds, shillings and pence were abandoned, the monetary unit has been the Australian dollar (abbreviated $ or $A), divided into 100 cents. There are coins of 1, 2, 5, 10, 20 and 50 cents and $1. Banknotes come in denominations of $2, $5, $10, $20, $50 and $100; the dimensions of the notes increase according to their face value. You can bring with you as much Australian or foreign currency as you wish, and on departure you can take away $5000 in local currency.

Changing money: Exchange rates fluctuate daily. Traveller's cheques and foreign currency may be changed at most banks in Australia with a minimum of fuss. Normal banking hours are 9.30 a.m. to 4 p.m. Monday to Thursday, till 5 p.m. Friday. In addition, in big cities the main downtown banks are open for foreign currency transactions as early as 8 a.m. and as late as 6 p.m. Some states charge a small tax for each transaction. Many hotels will change money at all hours, but the rate tends to be unfavourable.

Credit cards: The well-known international charge cards are recognized most places tourists go; look for their signs displayed at the entrance to a store or restaurant.

NEWSPAPERS AND MAGAZINES

More than 500 newspapers are published in Australia, from internationally esteemed big city dailies like the *Sydney Morning Herald* and *The Age* of Melbourne to backwoods weeklies. Among them are local periodicals aimed at the immigrant communities, written in Dutch, French, German, Greek, Italian and other languages. In the biggest cities specialist newsstands sell airmail copies of newspapers from London, Rome and Paris (including the *International Herald Tribune*) as well as weekly and monthly American and European magazines.

P PHOTOGRAPHY

There's so much to focus on that you'll probably run out of film. No problem, though: internationally known brands are sold everywhere in Australia. Quick-processing establishments are found in all the cities.

In the desert and the tropics keep your camera and film out of the hot sun, and beware of both sand and moisture.

Aborigines sometimes do not like having their photos taken— ask before you aim.

Wildlife is a fascinating subject, but it's only prudent to keep your distance when, for example, crocodiles or wild boar appear in the viewfinder. And buffalo can be much more dangerous than they appear.

POLICE

Each state operates its own police force, covering both urban and rural areas. The federal police force has jurisdiction over government property, including airports.

The emergency telephone number is 000.

PRICES

To give you an idea of what to expect, here are some average prices in Australian dollars. However, these can only be approximate in view of the problem of inflation. And prices differ from state to state and region to region.

Air fares. Sydney–Adelaide–Sydney economy $438, "See Australia" fare $306; Melbourne–Sydney–Cairns economy $678, "See Australia" $476.

Airport transfer. Sydney airport to city, coach: $2, taxi: $9. Melbourne airport to city, coach: $5, taxi: $18.

Car hire. Economy (unlimited kilometres): $35–$45 per day, $210–270 per week; business class $48–$70 per day, $290–$420 per week; luxury class $82–250 per day, $500-$1500 per week. Monthly rates are also available.

Cigarettes. Australian $1.80 for 20, $2.20–2.50 for 30; imported similar prices.

Bus tour. Half day $20, full day $40.

Hairdressers. *Ladies'* haircut $25, shampoo and set $15. *Men's* cut: $10.

Hotels. Luxury double $90 to $150 per night; medium $45 to $90; budget $5 to $45.

Meals and drinks. In a moderate restaurant, lunch $20, dinner $30. Bottle of wine (from bottle shop) $4 to $15, beer $1.80–$2, soft drink $1.20.

Nightlife. Nightclub, cover charge or minimum $8–$10; concert $25; theatre $20; cinema $8.

Taxis. Sydney, Circular Quay to Kings Cross $7; Melbourne, Flinders St. Station to Victorian Market $5.

Trains. Sydney–Brisbane first-class $87, berth $120, economy $62; Melbourne–Adelaide first-class $62, berth $95, economy $44.

RADIO AND TV R
Government-funded stations of the Australian Broadcasting Commission (ABC) and the Special Broadcasting Service (SBS) compete with a range of commercially run stations. Sydney and Melbourne have five television channels each, operating from 6 a.m. to midnight or later. The SBS stations are devoted to "multi-cultural" programmes, primarily in foreign languages with English subtitles. The big cities have a profusion of AM and FM radio stations for all tastes. The output of ABC-FM is almost entirely composed of classical music. Short-wave listeners can pick up Radio Australia (the overseas service of the ABC) and other long-range broadcasters such as the Voice of America, BBC World Service and Asian stations.

RELIGIOUS SERVICES
The majority religion in Australia is Christianity. The biggest denominations are Anglican (Church of England) and Roman Catholic, followed by Uniting Church, Presbyterian, Orthodox, Lutheran and Baptist. The Jewish, Islamic and Buddhist faiths are also represented. To find the church of your choice check at your hotel or look in the telephone directory under *Churches and Synagogues*.

RESTAURANTS (see also pp. 209–216)
Hearty eats are an important part of the Australian way of life—a lucky coincidence, considering the high quality of the ingredients available from coast to coast.

235

Restaurants come as classy as you can afford, with linen and candlelight and formally dressed waiters at the top of the market; there are plenty of pizzas and hamburgers for economy class. Between the extremes are some fine happy-medium establishments offering wholesome steaks and roasts, memorable seafood, or ethnic food from almost everywhere. Pub lunches are often good, and fast if you're rushed; a blackboard announces the choices of the day. The big cities usually have food centres in shopping arcades or the basements of office buildings, featuring a remarkable variety of fast-food counters, including vegetarian and ethnic specialities. Oriental food is a good bet: Sydney and Melbourne enjoy full-scale Chinatowns, and every other city also has its Chinese restaurants. New Vietnamese and other Indochinese restaurants reflect recent population trends.

The complicated licensing laws governing the sale of beverages vary from state to state. Some restaurants are licensed to serve wine, beer and spirits but many more are unlicensed. The latter allow, even encourage, you to "Bring Your Own" bottles; "BYO" is the abbreviation prominently displayed. There is no corkage charge. Fortunately for wine-and-dine enthusiasts, an off-licence or liquor store can usually be found within a block or two of a BYO restaurant.

Meal times are conventional in Australia. In the cities, dinner is served from about 6 to 9 p.m., but small-town folk dine earlier. There is no service charge except on weekends and legal holidays, when a surcharge is added to restaurant bills to compensate the employees for working less desirable hours. Tipping is optional; for commendable service leave up to 10 per cent.

S SHOPPING (see also pp. 204–209)

Almost every Australian town now has a pedestrians-only shopping street, even if it's just a couple of blocks long, to compete with the suburban shopping centres. The bigger downtown shopping malls are rich in attractions—street entertainers, outdoor cafés, sculpture, decorative fountains—to complement the business at hand. In spite of the glamour, shopping hours in most towns are quite restricted. Generally, stores are open from 8.30 or 9 a.m. to 5 or 5.30 p.m. on weekdays except for one late shopping night when they close at 8 or 9 p.m., and on Saturdays until noon.

The big cities have comprehensive, world-class department stores as well as speciality shops. Largely because of high production costs there are very few bargains in Australia, but this shouldn't deter your window-shopping and souvenir procurement programme.

Abundant in shopping areas are duty-free shops catering to Australians planning trips abroad as well as foreign tourists heading home. You'll have to show your passport and air ticket. Prices tend to be lower than at the airport; comparison shopping is a wise policy.

TIME DIFFERENCES T

Australia is so big it needs three time zones to follow the sun: Eastern, Central and Western. These are delineated by state boundaries. Complicating the situation, Central time is only half an hour earlier than Eastern, and daylight saving time occurs (but not in all states) in the northern hemisphere's winter. The chart covers the period from March to October when Australia is on standard time.

New York	London (GMT + 1)	Perth	Adelaide Darwin	Sydney Melbourne
7 a.m.	noon	7 p.m.	8.30 p.m.	9 p.m.

TIPPING

For most foreigners the Australian view of tipping takes some getting used to. Virtually no one in the service sector of the economy expects to be tipped. Nobody's livelihood depends on tips. A gratuity is optional, a reward for good service but not a requirement.

In hotels frequented by foreigners, porters are accustomed to receiving tips. In good restaurants a tip of 5 to 10 per cent is a just reward for efficient, courteous service. Taxi drivers accept but don't expect tips. In fact, drivers have been known to round *down* the fare to the nearest convenient sum. But it won't hurt any feelings if you *do* give an appreciative tip.

TOILETS

Australians manage without euphemisms for "toilet", though you may come across slang synonyms. The facilities are often distinguished by the letters "M" and "F" for Male and Female. Public conveniences usually adhere to a high standard of cleanliness and comfort, even in the Outback.

237

TOURIST INFORMATION OFFICES

Some overseas offices of Tourism Australia (the Australian Tourist Commission):

U.S.A.: Suite 467, 630 5th Ave., New York, N.Y. 10111-0043; tel. (212) 489-7500. Suite 1610, 3550 Wilshire Blvd., Los Angeles, CA 90010-2480; tel. (213) 380-6060.

U.K.: 4th Floor, Heathcoat House, 20 Savile Row, London W1X 1AE; tel. (01) 439-2773.

New Zealand: 15th Floor, Quay Tower, 29 Customs St. West, Auckland; tel. (09) 799594.

Singapore: 8th Floor, Orchard Towers, 400 Orchard Rd; tel. 235-2295.

Japan: Sankaido Building 7F, 9-13 Akasaka 1-Chome, Minato-ku, Tokyo 107; tel. (03) 585-0705.

Within Australia, each state operates its own tourist authority, with branch offices in most other capital cities. Each office is full of booklets, maps and information, and can help you with arrangements for travel and accommodation.

TRANSPORT

Domestic flights. Air traffic is exceptionally well developed, with more than 10 million passengers a year flying the domestic airlines across Australia's vastness. Two companies, Ansett Airlines and the state-owned Australian Airlines, compete on most of the important routes. Between Sydney and Melbourne, for instance, there may be a choice of 30 jet flights a day. Regional airlines round out the busy aerial network. It's wise to make advance reservations, particularly during the busy school holiday periods. Although domestic air fares are high, tourists from overseas are entitled to big discounts; but the packages may involve rigid itineraries. Well-informed travel agents can supply details of the latest deals.

Trains. Intercity train travel in Australia can be a great adventure—so fascinating for rail buffs that reservations may be hard to come by. The legendary trains involve desert journeys between Adelaide and Alice Springs (the Ghan) and between Sydney and Perth (the Indian-Pacific). Nowadays modern air-conditioned trains with sleeping compartments, showers, dining cars and club cars cover these gruelling routes in comfort. Advance reservations—up to 12 months in advance—are especially recommended for the Indian-Pacific linking ocean to ocean as well as certain long-distance routes in Queensland. On a more prosaic level, trains cover shorter-range interstate and commuter runs. Ask your travel agent about money-saving rail passes, in first or economy class, for foreign tourists.

Intercity buses. Express coaches, often luxuriously equipped, link all the main population centres. For unhurried travellers who want to see Australia close up, at a reasonable price, the main coach companies offer special bargain deals, for instance two weeks or a month of unlimited mileage at fixed rates. Some of the packages must be purchased before you arrive in Australia.

Local transport. In the big cities, you can hail a **taxi** on the street if its roof sign reads "Vacant". Otherwise you can go to one of the cab stands, usually found at shopping centres, transport terminals and big hotels. You can also phone for a taxi. Meters indicate the fare plus any extras, such as waiting time. A courtesy note: Australians usually sit next to the taxi driver; if you don't, you might be considered unfriendly.

Local **bus** service tends to be concentrated during business hours; in many towns it tapers off after dark. To encourage car drivers to avoid downtown traffic and parking problems, some cities provide free buses from the periphery. There are also special tickets valid for unlimited public transport travel for two hours or a whole day.

Melbourne is proud of its **trams** (streetcars), which provide an efficient grid of downtown and suburban lines. The tracks, running down the middle of the street, are also used effectively by emergency vehicles. Melbourne also has an **underground** railway system (subway), as do Sydney and Brisbane.

Ferries are a vital part of life in Sydney, where so many commuters cross the harbour. The ferries, concentrated at Circular Quay, also provide cheap outings for sightseers.

WATER
Yes, you can drink the water from any tap in Australia, unless it is specifically marked otherwise. In the Outback, warnings might read "Bore water" or "Not for drinking."

WEIGHTS AND MEASURES

Since the 1960s Australia has adhered to the metric system. Old-timers may still reckon distances in miles but generally the abandonment of British Imperial measures is total. Some standard conversions:

Temperature

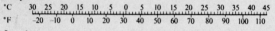

Length

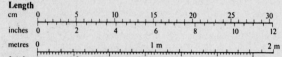

Weight

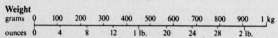

Fluid measures

imp.gals. scale

litres scale

U.S.gals. scale

Kilometres to miles

km	0	1	2	3	4	5	6	8	10	12	14	16
miles	0	½	1	1½	2	3	4	5	6	7	8	9	10

Y YOUTH HOSTELS

Young backpackers can find cheap lodgings in more than 100 youth hostels all over Australia. You should have a membership card from the Youth Hostel Association in your home country. Information may be obtained from the Australian Youth Hostel Association, 60 Mary St., Surrey Hills, N.S.W. 2010; tel. (02) 212-1151.

Another source of inexpensive accommodation: university residence halls. Rooms are available, with or without meals, during vacation periods—May, August, and from late November to the end of February.

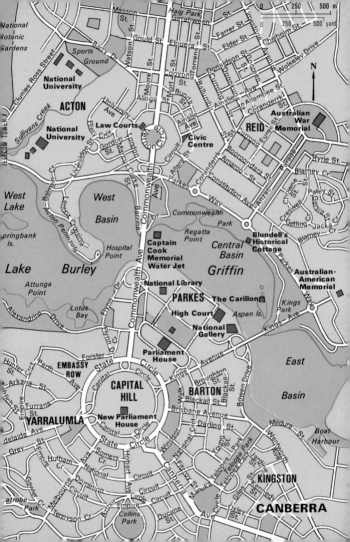

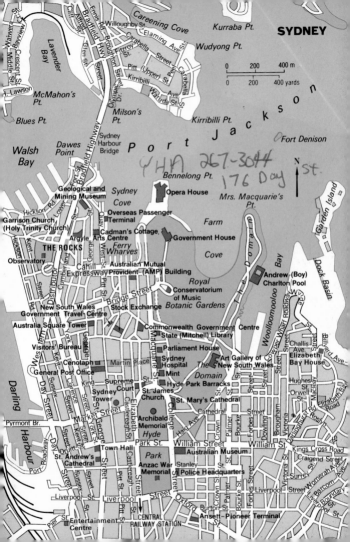

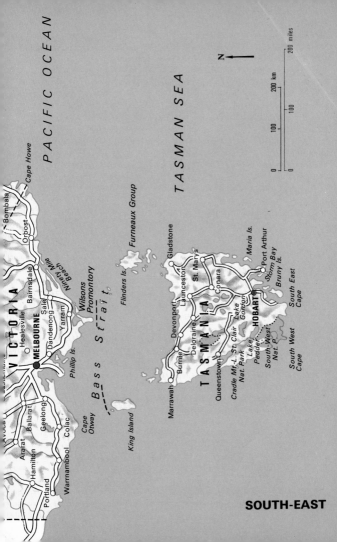

SOUTH-EAST

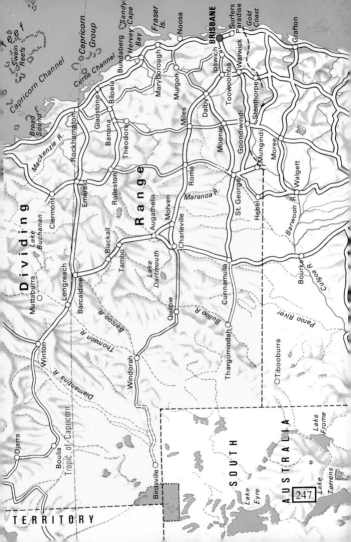

NORTHERN   TERRITORY

Lake
Argyle

Drysdale River Nat. Park

Wyndham

Gibb River

Halls Creek

Lake White

Lake Hazlett

Lake Mackay

Lake Macdonald

Gregory Salt Lake

Great   Sandy   Desert

Fitzroy R.

Fitzroy Crossing

Collier Bay

King Sound

Derby

Cape Leveque

Tropic of Capricorn

Gibson

Percival Lakes

Lake Auld

Rudall River Nat. Park

Broome

Lake Disappointment

N

200 miles

200 km

100

100

INDIAN

Eighty Mile Beach

Oakover River

Great

0

OCEAN

Port Hedland

Chichester Range Nat. Park

Collier Range

Roebourne

Hamersley Range Nat. Park

Hamersley Range

Ashburton R.

Barrow Island

Onslow

Lake Kennedy

Exmouth

WESTERN AUSTRALIA

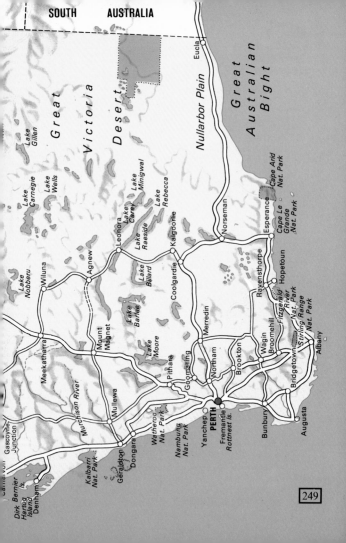

SOUTH AUSTRALIA

Great Victoria Desert

Nullarbor Plain

Great Australian Bight

Eucla

Cape Arid Nat. Park

Esperance
Cape Le Grande Nat. Park

Norseman

Lake Minigwal
Lake Rebecca
Lake Carey
Leonora
Lake Raeside
Kalgoorlie

Coolgardie

Lake Wells
Lake Carnegie

Agnew

Lake Nobberu

Wiluna

Lake Barlee

Lake Ballard

Lake Moore

Mount Magnet

Ravensthorpe

Hopetoun
Fitzgerald River Nat. Park

Broomehill
Wagin

Stirling Range Nat. Park

Merredin

Pithara
Goomalling
Wongan
Northam
Brookton

Bridgetown

Albany

Meekatharra

Murchison River

Mullewa

Wheatbelt

Watheroo Nat. Park

Nambung Nat. Park

Yanchep
PERTH
Fremantle
Rottnest Is.

Bunbury

Augusta

Dongara
Geraldton

Kalbarri Nat. Park

Dirk Hartog Is.
Bernier Is.
Denham
Gascoyne Junction

249

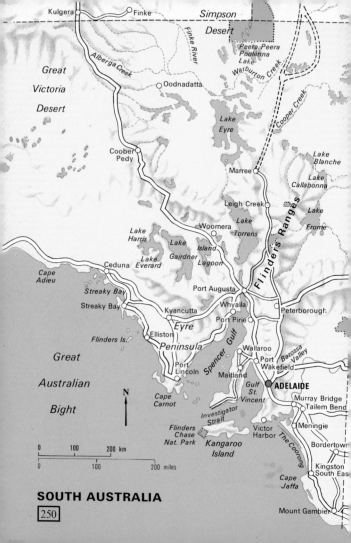

SOUTH AUSTRALIA

250

INDEX

An asterisk (*) next to a page number indicates a map reference. Where there is more than one set of page references, the one in bold type refers to the main entry. For index to Practical Information, see pp. 218–219.